Did I Really Mean to Buy a Horse

What to Do When Your Horse Is Acting
Like a Monster, and When (and How)
to Call for Help

Why Does My Horse Act Like This?

The Well-Mannered Horse

Meredith Hill

Contents

The Well-Mannered Horse
Developing an Ideal Equine Buddy

Download your free checklist now!

If you've ever checked out an equine supply website or stopped by a
tack shop, you might find your head swimming regarding
all of the stuff people buy to help them care for their horses. How do
you decide what you need to buy?
I've created this checklist to help new horse owners get organized right
from the start.
Go to https://free.meredithhillbook.com/checklist to download it for
free

Why Does My Horse Act Like This?

Understanding Equine Behavior in your New Horse

Meredith Hill

Contents

Introduction

Once upon a time, there was a little child who was obsessed with horses. Many of the people reading that sentence can likely identify with that sentiment, but in the case of this child, the obsession just continued to blossom and grow as she read absolutely everything she could find with "horse" in the title.

Eventually, this child became a grownup, and after over a decade of reading books and taking riding lessons, she got her own horse. As the years went by, she decided she needed to be around horses as much as possible, so she got involved in equine rescue, did some training, worked at a whole lot of different barns, tried as many different riding styles as possible, and kept learning, learning, and learning.

This child, of course, is me, and I am delighted to be back with another installment of horse books for readers like you. After releasing my first book, *Before Your Horse Comes Home: Introductory Horse Care for Beginners,* I started getting emails from folks just like you who wanted to know more about horses and my perspective on certain issues they were having. First, may I say please don't stop writing– I love engaging with all of you! But what I noticed is that a lot of folks aren't quite sure why horses behave the way they do.To be perfectly honest, there are a lot of experts with far more saddle and training time than myself who still wonder why horses act as they do. When people ask me what horses are like, I often compare their overall demeanor to a chaotic cross between a human toddler and a house cat. Boisterous, yet mysterious. Energetic, yet opinionated. Wanting to cuddle while simultaneously not wanting to be touched. Accident-prone and just intelligent enough to get into trouble without knowing how to get out of it. Oh yeah, and they weigh a thousand pounds (give or take) and can move at speeds of up to 40 miles per hour.

When I blurt out this assessment to people with limited exposure to horses, they generally make a face that tells me they will never interact with a horse on purpose, and that they are also concerned for my sanity and safety. I get it – horses are scary. They are intimidating and dangerous... unless you know what you're doing, and more importantly, why they are acting the way they do.

While I recommend that anyone who works with or wants to work with horses read this book, I would like to stress that knowing why a horse is doing whatever nonsense they're doing does not automatically equip you to march out there and retrain it. Refer back a few sentences to the "intimidating and dangerous" part. They have big teeth, and tough jaws, and they can use any or all of their hooves to strike you from a variety of directions. The first rule of working with horses on a professional level is, "never trust a new horse." That rule has kept many of us alive.

That doesn't mean equine professionals are without battle scars. Between handling and riding rescue horses, I've had an abundance of injuries that have ranged from minor to "had to take time off work." In fact, I'll never forget the time I showed up at a presentation for a new client in my very fancy corporate days, sporting an impressive black eye from pulling a panicked rescue horse out of a wire fence the night before. Or the time I showed up for a date covered in blood from working with a pasture broodmare who had never been handled by humans.

I know it's futile to say this, but don't let these things scare you. Working with horses is like any new activity. You're not going to be great at first. You need to learn and practice and grow. You will need a professional to help guide you through the process. So, while I'm here to give you the background on the hows and whys of horse behavior, I strongly urge you to work with a local professional to at least give you eyes on the ground that your ideas and methods aren't going to land you in urgent care.

Trainers, cowboys, and horse behaviorists are some of the most sought-after equine professionals for exactly this reason, and I recommend researching your local resources. But fear not— we'll go through all of the things to look for when choosing a professional to help you. And, as always, I've got a Resources section tucked at the end to help you continue to learn more about equine behavior.

I also listened to your feedback about using too many "horsey" terms, and I respect that. No one is born knowing everything! Therefore, I have endeavored to explain things in detail as I go to reduce any confusion. Most of the topics I cover are included in the Resources section, so if you find you still have some questions, check out the corresponding Resources.

Bear in mind, I am not claiming to be the ultimate source of knowledge when it comes to horse behavior. Think of me more as your buddy who has done a lot of research on the topic and is happy to swap stories with you. I've worked with stallions, mares, and geldings alike—some feral, some abused or mistreated, some well-trained and polite, and some who were absolute jerks. Working with each one is a completely different experience, and what worked on one had absolutely no impact on another. These creatures have their own personalities, histories, and understanding of what we teach them.

What I hope to do in the coming pages is share with you some of the basics of a few of the weird things that horses do, and theories as to why these behaviors happen. Knowing why can often help us figure out how to help the horse consider another behavior instead. If we're lucky, they choose to do what we wanted them to do in the first place. But more often than not, it's a matter of compromise for both parties.

If you are currently filled with trepidation, don't be. The likelihood of encountering a horse that does all of the things I mention in this book is surprisingly low. And, if you're reading this book as you prepare to enter the world of horses, I want to make it abundantly clear that around 90% of the horses you'll meet in a lesson setting will be mild-mannered good citizens who enjoy a life of praise, petting, and post-ride treats. For those who are in the process of horse shopping, the details in this book can give you some insight into things to look for in a prospective partner, as well.

No matter how deeply connected or obsessed you are with horses, I hope this book helps you understand and appreciate these nonsensical, beautiful, amazing, ridiculous creatures a bit more.

Chapter One

Evolution, Instinct, and How Horses Behave in the Wild

To understand horses, we need to understand where horses came from. This may sound cliche, but horses are actually a relatively recent addition to the world of domestication.

Geneticists, historians, archaeologists, and forensic scientists have been working to pinpoint where horses arrived on the timeline of human evolution—I've included a few links in the Resources section in case you're as curious as I am—but many feel that horses became a regular part of human life as work animals and transportation between 2500 and 2000 BCE. Comparatively, experts believe dogs were likely domesticated between 30,050 and 17,050 BCE.

Therefore, even though your horse or pony may have never seen anything more exotic than a dirt pen, they still aren't that far removed from pure, primordial instinct. I encourage people to remember this when working with horses because it's very easy to let yourself believe that "domesticated" means "trained". Horses are born with instincts to get away from predators and fight any threat they cannot outrun. They are not born with the understanding of what being haltered and led around means, and they have absolutely no idea what a saddle is until they're properly introduced.

I'd like to start by sharing the history of how today's modern domesticated horses came to be to help you understand how some of their instincts may have developed. I'll also share how today's feral horses act and react. Then we'll compare that to the lifestyle of domesticated horses. You might be surprised to recognize your own horse's eccentricities in this quick history lesson!

How a Horse Became a Horse

I want to preface this part by noting that this is not a comprehensive guide to equine evolution. Many resources can break this topic into a dissertation-level discussion. Still, to understand the behavior of the modern horse, I don't feel that level of detail is necessary. It is, however, absolutely fascinating, and I recommend checking it out when you get a chance.

Furthermore, science is still making discoveries regarding early mammals. Originally, it was thought that horses were introduced to North America by early colonists from Europe. However, archaeological evidence has demonstrated that *Eohippus*, the "dawn horse," was a literal globe trotter, with thousands of complete fossils discovered in Europe and North America alike. Fossils of early horses have also been found in South America and western to central Asia.

The earliest equids hardly resemble their modern ancestors. *Eohippus* is largely considered to be the very first horse, with fossils dating back to about 52 million years ago. It definitely wouldn't make a good riding buddy, and you might need to call a small animal trainer first. Standing approximately between a foot and a foot and a half in height, *Eohippus* wasn't much larger than many breeds of dog. Furthermore, instead of the large solid hooves that we're accustomed to today, this pint-size pony had five hooved toes at the end of each leg.

You might be wondering how we're absolutely certain that *Eohippus* was actually a horse. It turns out that these slender-legged grazing animals were built with hind legs slightly longer than the front, which aided them in running swiftly through thick forests and grasslands. They traveled in herds and roamed throughout their territory in search of food.

Fast forward about 20 million years and early horses start to look more like the ponies we see today. They still had multiple toes, but they were larger and faster, with long necks to help them graze and browse for food in forests and mountainous regions.

Horses hung onto their extra toes until about 5 million years ago when their longer legs developed one strong toe instead of multiple digits. Their roaming lifestyle and diet rich in plant protein helped them grow taller, with stronger muscles to help them run more and more swiftly from their many predators.

You can see evidence of the horse's evolution when you look at the inside of its legs. Along the forearm and gaskin (the part of the leg between the body and the knee or hock), you'll find a rough patch of what feels like skin. Today we call that part of the horse's anatomy the "chestnut."

We've discovered along the way that chestnuts grow in a unique shape and form, like fingerprints on humans. Some breed registries include photos of a horse's chestnut pattern to identify each individual horse.

The ergot is a similar holdover from the early days of Equus. Located at the back of the joint just above the hoof, known as the fetlock, some horses have no ergot protrusion, while others have something that almost resembles a cat or dog's dewclaw. The principle is the same in each—a vestigial toe that just hasn't left the species yet.

So why are we focusing so closely on the horse's feet? A common theory among enthusiasts and equine biologists is that if a horse's foot still has reminders of the species' evolution, then it stands to reason that some of the horse's instincts are holdovers from 52 million years ago, as well.

Obviously, we can't really understand how an *Eohippus* would act. What we can do is study fossils and recreate the environment in which this little guy lived. We can figure out what they ate, where they lived, and who their predators were. From that, we can deduce that a five-toed beast standing around a foot tall was prepared, both physically and mentally, to run for its life. Some argue that horses grew taller not only because of richer nutrition but so they could more easily spot predators. Their necks grew longer so they could continue to graze as their legs got longer, and their backs developed from the narrow, flat style we see on zebras and Przewalski's horses into defined, muscular hindquarters and broad shoulders for additional speed and stamina.

Horses' bodies evolved for physical survival. But what about their mental development? Which equine instincts might be lurking deep within your horse's DNA?

The urge to run away from things that are threatening is obvious, but let's keep brainstorming. What about a horse's teeth? Most horses will bite before they kick. Looking at the shape of a horse, this makes sense. With their long necks, they can reach along both sides of their body, up, down, and forward to sink their teeth into potential danger. They can also telescope that neck out in all of those directions to find food. And, with their very large, surprisingly dexterous upper lips, horses are very good at finding what they want and bringing it to them for consumption or closer examination.

Horses' eyes have developed on the sides of their head so that they can almost see all the way around their body. Their "blind spots", so to speak, are right in front of their nose and behind their rear end. Those long necks also enable horses to turn their heads to expand their field of vision. Their eyes are very sensitive to motion. If a horse sees something out of the corner of its eye, it will often turn its head in that direction, perk up its ears to hear more clearly, and flare its nostrils to catch the scent of whatever monster might be lurking in the shadows.

Rearing and bucking probably developed many millions of years ago, as well. When horses rear, they stand up on their hind legs to seem big and intimidating. It usually works, especially because from this stance, horses can kick out with their front legs to keep danger at bay, or even fling themselves backward to avoid an attack.

Bucking, on the other hand, is when a horse strikes out with both of its hind feet. Those big hindquarter muscles that help horses run fast also pack a punch going the other direction. A bucking horse puts its head down and launches its hindquarters up violently, so bucking likely developed as a way for horses to get predators off their backs. They often drop a shoulder, too, to swing the offender off to the side. Kicking is similar to bucking but is generally a one-time punt type of action. A horse kicks to get something out of its periphery. Horse bucks to get rid of what they believe to be an assailant.

Furthermore, there's the herd instinct. We'll talk about this a lot more in a bit but know that your horse was not designed to live alone. Early horses found safety in numbers, and domesticated and wild horses today still generally prefer to live in groups. In my career, I've encountered only one horse who preferred to live alone, and he was more than adequately prepared to defend himself through any means possible. He was also entirely too clever and could figure out how to open nearly any door or gate and jump any fence. Without a herd, a horse has to keep himself alive on his own instincts, which can result in some unpleasant behavior that we'll discuss.

While a lot of the evolution of instinct is deduced through understanding the lifestyle and environment of early horses, it is very clear that the species survived because it was able to defend itself and run away from its predators. Even though evolutionary evidence is discovered every day, thus updating and changing our lingering theories, we can all agree that, he who does not get eaten lives longer. Therefore, the 12-inch tall *Eohippus* and all of its descendants have not only learned how to live longer but have passed this information down in the form of instinct.

It's often hard to remember how very feral horses still are, especially when we watch them get super-excited about their favorite treat, or when they nicker warmly as we approach them. However, deep down inside, each horse carries the instinct of a small forest-dwelling creature who simply did not want to get eaten. And that is why we proceed with care when working with today's horses, *Equus caballus*.

Self-Care, Wild Horse Style

When we think of today's horses, we often think of our pony friends who live comfortably in their stalls, lounge in lush green fields, and bring joy to the lives of countless humans. But of the estimated 7.2 million horses worldwide, around 600,000 live in the wild.

90,000 of those horses roam freely around the American West. Technically speaking, they are not "wild" horses, since they are descendants of horses who escaped domestication during the early days of colonization. During the Western Expansion, horses similarly found themselves without human companionship, due to accidents, catastrophes, or simply running like the wind in a land that had no fences. Therefore, these horses are frequently referred to as "feral" or "free-roaming" to make the distinction from the horses worldwide who have never experienced domestication. Technically speaking once again, the Przewalski's Horse of Mongolia is the only living truly wild horse breed. All other herds have been traced to domesticated ancestors.

The American Mustang is a fascinating animal with rich history, and I've had the pleasure of encountering several of these horses both in the wild and in the barn. The US Bureau of Land Management (BLM) National Wild Horse and Burro Advisory Board watches out for these truly feral horses, who roam 32.6 million acres of land ranging from Oregon to Wyoming, and Northern Montana to Southern California and Arizona. Nevada is particularly dense with herds, though the BLM also tracks herds in Idaho, Colorado, Utah, and New Mexico.

If wild and feral horse herds intrigue you, I've included some links in the Resources section so you can dive deeper into the topic.

With these statistics in mind, the fact that horses still roam in the wild and manage to survive without monthly vet bills, farrier work, expensive supplements, and fully balanced feed continues to confuse people. It's a valid question– how *do* horses keep themselves alive in the wild, while we dig deeper and deeper into our pockets to help our domesticated equine companions stay healthy and happy?

The simplest answer is that wild horses have one job– to stay alive. Everything about their behavior, habits, physique, and instincts has developed around that single goal.

Most wild horses are not particularly large; in fact, many can be classified as "ponies", since they stand less than 14.2 hands high. A horse is measured from its withers – the prominent bony point where the neck and shoulder meet– to the ground. A "hand" is four inches; therefore, a "pony" measures less than 58 inches from its withers to the ground.

The reason feral equines are so small is a sheer matter of food availability. Smaller ponies need less food. Even then, "wild" horses spend approximately 17-18 hours grazing each day. If you've ever spent time in the areas of the American West where Mustangs roam, you'll know that it's not exactly lush pasture ground. The land itself features wide, seemingly barren plains interrupted by mountains and canyons. The ground is rocky, and where the soil turns to sand, there are few trees for shelter or eating.

Therefore, to consume enough vegetation to survive, Mustangs need to move around a lot. Generally speaking, a feral horse will travel between 10 and 20 miles each day to ensure they have enough food and water. This not only benefits them nutritionally, but physically as well.

First, there's the matter of their hooves. Horse hooves are made of keratin, just like our fingers- and toenails. Walking, trotting, and occasionally galloping across sandy and rocky terrain has a similar effect to using a nail file on our own nails. Furthermore, wild horses have adapted to this type of environment with much stronger hooves than their domesticated cousins.

Remember also that wild horses don't have a side hustle, like domesticated horses. They aren't ridden in a frame and they don't pull or haul anything. They mostly walk and graze, exerting themselves in bursts of speed only when they really need to. As a result, they don't tend to have the same performance-related musculoskeletal issues we find in domesticated horses, such as arthritis, sore backs, and damaged tendons. That's not to say that wild horses don't have these issues; it's simply that the prognosis is far grimmer when your survival depends on your ability to move quickly. While domesticated horses typically live to age 30 and beyond, wild horse life expectancy is more like 15 to 20 years.

Experts are still working to understand how the lifestyle of wild horses can contribute to their overall health and wellness. The fact that they have access to a far wider range of plant materials seems to point to an instinct to know what's good to eat, and what to avoid. Is it possible that horses intuitively know what to eat to help maintain wellness? Can we learn more about the huge enigma that is the equine digestive process by observing wild horses' grazing patterns? At this time this concept is not completely understood, but experts are working to get a better grasp on it.

Another fascinating phenomenon that experts continue to study in free-roaming horses is their herd behavior. I am personally fascinated by herd behavior and the seemingly random process by which horses choose who their buddies are, who's in charge, and the various roles and responsibilities found within each herd.

Herd instinct comes from the concept of safety in numbers. Since early horse fossils were generally found in groups, scientists have theorized that horses have been herd animals since the beginning. As a result, this instinct is likely deeply hard-wired into each equine critter we meet, regardless of their domestication situation.

Typically, a herd is led by a stallion or adult male horse. Herds generally do not have more than one stallion, so any offspring between the stallion and his band of female horses, called "mares", will be related through the paternal line. Therefore, once male babies, or colts, reach a certain age, they have a great big blowout fight with Dad over the rights to the herd. Most of the time, this results in banishment, so the Colts trot off with a bruised ego to form a bachelor herd of single guys who don't know where to go. Over time, these guys start stealing mares from existing herds, oftentimes by fighting that herd's stallion and new herds are formed.

Stallions aren't just glorified baby daddies– they have a lot of work to do to keep the herd functioning properly. A herd's stallion is mostly responsible for guiding everyone to sustenance, as well as protecting them from any potential danger. I say "mostly", because they often have assistance.

In some cases, a herd will include an alpha stallion who serves as the CEO of the herd– he's the big guy to whom everyone answers. However, there are sometimes a few other stallions hanging around to help keep things in order. They don't have the same level of power and assertion, but they can be helpful in the alpha stallion's defense strategies.

And then there are the "boss mares". This isn't just a colloquialism for a woman in charge– it quite literally is the term used to describe the highest-ranking mares in a herd. They typically take over the administrative duties of the alpha stallion, making sure each member of the herd goes where they should, does what they should, and doesn't start any trouble.

Then there's everyone else. Bear in mind, there are no geldings—a common term for a castrated male horse—in the wild, except for those who ended up roaming free unintentionally. Therefore, the rest of the herd includes mares of every age, as well as foals and yearlings who are not quite ready to head out on their own.

Each herd has to sort out its own social hierarchy. Mares will pick on each other or even fight to earn status within a herd. Out come the teeth, and hooves go flying as they physically enforce who is most dominant within the herd. With dominance comes reward, such as first access to the best grazing and water sources. Herd dynamics are not always pleasant. Sometimes members of a herd are completely banished or left behind, which means they'll need to find a new herd to survive. Unfortunately, finding a new herd means establishing the pecking order once again.

But things aren't always nasty within the herd. Wild horses are often found participating in mutual grooming, using their teeth to gently nibble on each others' necks and backs. Herd members will also defend each other—especially younger and weaker members—when they sense danger. They often find close companions within their herds and travel closely with their buddies.

Horses communicate with each other in many different ways. The position of a stallion's ears can tell the herd that something weird is going on, and they need to be instantly alert. Raising the head and showing the whites of their eyes says, "Stay back, buddy, or there will be trouble!" What we might consider subtle body languages, such as a swivel of the ear or a flick of the tail, can mean some very important things between two horses.

As an equine professional, studying herd dynamics has helped me understand some very important things about how horses communicate with each other and with humans. I'm not an expert by any stretch, and my observations go no further than the back fields of a variety of carefully-manicured barns and stables, but watching horses interact with each other can tell us a lot about what they expect from those who share their space. Furthermore, knowing what "that face" means can be incredibly helpful in getting insight into your horse's strange behaviors.

Unfortunately, as humans, we tend to expect the horse to learn what our words and actions mean without taking the time to understand their language. Next time you get the chance, I urge you to pause and watch a group of horses interact with each other. Play the role of the passive bystander, and don't try to get them to "do" anything. Instead, just watch what they do. Notice how they place their bodies in relation to each other, as well as any other surrounding points of interest, like that huge field over there, or that place where they once saw a deer. You may notice one horse is intently surveying the landscape while the rest of the herd grazes with fervor. Are some horses lying down, enjoying a nice snooze while another keeps an eye out for danger? Are they nipping and squealing at each other when they want a turn at the water trough? All of these are very natural methods of communication for horses, and like any other language, the more you immerse yourself in it, the more it will start to make sense. After all, they're just horses, doing horse things, the way they were intended.

Challenges of Domestication

I would like to make it abundantly clear that I'm not against domestication. In fact, I am very aware that neither my Quarter Horse mare, Belle, nor my Thoroughbred gelding, Red, stands a chance in the wild. It's an exceedingly bad idea to run around setting modern domesticated horses free because they frequently lack the functional features Mustangs have developed over time. Also, your neighbors will be really upset about what happens to their lawns after a few horses have grazed on them for a day or two.

At the same time, it is worth noting for the topic of this book that domestication has presented certain physical and mental challenges in maintaining horse health. Thankfully, science, agriculture, and sheer human determination have helped us come up with viable solutions for any shortcomings between how horses evolved to live, and how they live today in modern barns and stables.

Most of us don't have a property that spans 10-20 miles, nor do we have the resources to maintain a full herd of horses. The golden standard is one acre of pasture per horse, but with current zoning and land availability, many of us have to turn out horses on a rotating schedule, rather than letting them graze for 17-18 hours per day. I have encountered barns that offered this capability, and I absolutely agree the horses benefited from it.

To get a sense of what living in a stall is like, consider locking yourself in your bathroom for a full day. A couple of times a day, someone will come by and give you food and make sure you haven't done anything disgusting to your water supply. Then they might let you out of the bathroom to run around in the living room for a few hours before putting you back in the bathroom. They might also take you outside and *force* you to run around for a bit.

Some people would be absolutely fine with this prospect. A nice cozy place to chill out, no one bothers you most of the time, and you don't have to come up with your own food? To some folks, that could be ideal.

On the other hand, let's say you're the type of person who really likes to be doing things and know what's going on. And while you have a nice view from the bathroom, you can't really go anywhere, except for when people let you out to do the stuff you really love to do. You have all this energy, and you only get to let it out a few times a day.

Horses generally fall into these two categories, though just like humans, there are all sorts of opinions in between. Most of the horses I've met who have spent most of their lives in stalls are perfectly fine with the concept, as long as they get the opportunity to get out and express their equine emotions and stuff themselves with grass frequently enough to keep them happy.

The main thing I'd like everyone to understand about equine domestication is that horses bred in captivity are often bigger, stronger, yet more delicate physically than their feral cousins. But, the instinct that helps wild horses thrive on the plains also inspires the thought processes and reactions of the purebred, never-left-the-property version of an equine that lives in your barn.

To a very large extent, consistent and fair training will help horses learn new ways of processing information. For example, with some convincing, horses can learn to appreciate that a human will get on their back not because they want to eat them as a predator would, but because they want to go on fun adventures together. Horses can be convinced that plastic bags are not horse-eating demons and that the flag waving on the other side of the property is not a monster waiting to pounce.

I think a lot of horse people don't necessarily stop to consider the fact that what we call "training" is basically re-wiring a horse's instincts to suit our needs as humans. Granted, what we teach them about their actions and reactions also helps them survive and thrive in a modern, technological world. We introduce them to their barn environment. They learn where the gates are in the pastures, how troughs are placed, where humans typically bring their food, and what times of day to expect food. They know what traffic sounds like and what it means to be approached by humans. Humans and horses alike become accustomed to their surroundings, to the point where they can tune out things they hear, see, and experience throughout the day.

But that doesn't mean we can completely eliminate their instincts. My old Thoroughbred, Red, is a former racehorse. He wasn't very good in that role, so he only started in 9 races. However, in that amount of time, it appears he was exposed to everything under the sun. This horse has calmly dealt with so many potential catastrophes, that I'm tempted to call him bombproof. He stood patiently and received acupuncture for the first time in front of a radio broadcasting booth and dozens of people at an equine education event. He's walked in parades, given pony rides, done therapeutic work, and was nearly backed into by a trailer because he didn't feel like moving.

Except for one time: We were having a lesson with my trainer, standing in the middle of the outdoor arena while she explained a concept to us. Without warning, a motorized bicycle raced down the dirt road next to the barn, pulling behind it a mini-fridge that bounced, crashed, and rattled its way down the road. I felt Red tense up and saw his ears fly forward and back rapidly as he consulted his mental encyclopedia to see if he could identify this particular monster. He could not, and he spun quickly and bolted to get away from whatever this mystery attacker might be. I stayed with him and calmed him almost immediately, but that was the only time in our fifteen years of partnership I experienced a big spook from him. I didn't blame him because that was a strange and loud combination of objects that we'd never seen before and haven't seen since!

When horses have what we consider "behavioral problems," they're often exhibiting some type of instinct that does not serve them well in a domestic arrangement. They may not necessarily be trying to be "mean," but instead, they've decided that this situation is dangerous. They usually believe they are acting appropriately. When we train our horses, we are teaching them that what they believe to be perilous is actually quite safe. We're asking them to ignore their instincts and trust us, instead.

We also ask them to not act like horses. Instead of roaming all day, we expect them to stand politely in their stalls or remain in their pastures. As a result, many of the things we consider "naughty manners" are actually due to plain boredom.

I consider it an honor to build a partnership with a horse. I'm the type of person who prefers to establish what I consider a "working relationship" at minimum. Though I may not interact with them every day, if I'm cleaning a stall, handling or grooming a horse, or feeding it, I want to be sure we're both on the same page. If only for a moment, we've got to understand and trust each other so we can get through this situation safely. For many horses, these types of interactions are no big deal. They don't care if housekeeping comes in and tidies the stall while they're in it; they'll just hang out on the other side and munch on some hay. Other horses do not appreciate their privacy being interrupted and will react poorly to someone who doesn't follow what they consider to be the "proper" steps of interaction.

In nearly every situation, the cause of poor behavior has been due to instinct, pain, boredom, prior abuse, or lack of training. Some folks say "There are no bad horses," and I have to disagree. There are bad horses, but they are rarely born that way. Most horses can be persuaded to trust a human, but it's up to us to never betray that trust.

Now that you have some idea about how a horse's brain was designed and functions, you might have a few "aha!" moments about things you've seen your horse do. Perhaps you have a Boss Mare who has distinct ideas about where the herd should be at all times. Maybe you know a Bachelor herd of goofy male horses who seem to be constantly fighting. Most likely, you'll have a few moments in which your horse's body language starts to make a little more sense.

I like to say that learning to communicate with your horse is basically like learning a new language. Even as we teach our horses our human requests, we learn a little bit of the horse's language as well, in the form of body language and behavior. Knowing how horses have developed, where their instinct comes from, and why these instincts exist has provided me with plenty of insight as I continue to learn how to communicate with them. I hope this information will help you recognize some instinctive behavior in your horses as well.

Now that we have an idea of how horses' brains are wired and why, let's take a look at how the behaviors we consider "naughty" might actually be your horse's honest attempt to communicate important information to you.

Chapter Two

Causes of Naughtiness

It is a poorly-kept secret that horse people sometimes say things about their horses that they may not necessarily mean in general. However, in that particular moment of communication, trust, and growth, things have gone sideways, and they really and truly feel their horse is a jerk (or in other more colorful terms) in the heat of the moment.

Sometimes, this is very much warranted. Like humans, horses have a range of personalities, and, in my opinion, emotions or moods. Science is still working to find out how horses process emotions, but I contend that they have grumpy, happy, and excited days, just like we do. Surely you have had days where you didn't want to exercise, and you wanted to stay indoors and eat all day. What about those days when you start cleaning one part of your house, and suddenly you've spent all day mega-detailing every inch of your abode? Logic and behavior rarely walk in tandem.

However, before you decide to write your horse off as just a generally bad team player, it's a good idea to spend some time trying to determine if they're actually trying to tell you something, in their very big and dangerous sort of way.

As noted in the previous section, instinct is a huge part of why horses react the way they do. But what causes them to act that way in the first place? Most experienced horse folks believe that horses primarily act poorly because of pain, boredom, previous training (including no training at all), and/or something that has happened to them in the past. If you can eliminate all of these potential causes, then you can honestly classify your horse as a jerk– though you'll probably still love them, anyway.

It is very easy for us humans to forget these potential causes of naughtiness because we don't act that way. When we're in pain, we usually complain to someone, take a few over-the-counter pills, soak in a tub, throw on a lidocaine patch, or make an appointment with a specialist. When we're bored, we do something about it. If we don't know what we're doing, we ask questions, and if we're scared out of our wits…well, generally speaking, we have the same reactions as horses in that particular instance.

Horses can't ask questions or make plans with friends, and they definitely can't get the lid off of a bottle of over-the-counter pain medication without spilling the whole thing. Therefore, when things are going wrong for them, they have no choice but to tell us about it through their actions and reactions.

I feel each of these scenarios is important enough to warrant its own chapter, so bear with me as we dig a little deeper into each of these potential reasons why your horse might be acting naughty. I'll share what to look for and how you might be able to tell if each one could be the source of your horse's bratty behavior. Chances are you might recognize a few responses and reactions from each chapter!

Pain

When a horse who is otherwise kind and courteous starts acting like a fool, the first thing I want to find out is where it hurts. Very frequently, a horse who is suddenly violent, ill-mannered, or impolite is trying to explain that something painful is happening.

Unfortunately for them, horses are very large with many complicated, hidden parts. Furthermore, when we ask them what hurts, they cannot say, "Thanks for asking, human. It seems I have a pain right here," and they can't point to the source either. However, horses will do their best to tell us what's going on, as long as we're paying attention.

Many times you can find the source of pain by looking for swelling and heat. Bumps and bruises, tendon and ligament injuries, and musculoskeletal issues will often present with swollen, soft, tender tissue that is hot to the touch. Even abscesses of the hoof, which are internal to the keratin structure of the hoof, will result in swelling and heat in the affected leg.

If your horse is being a textbook jerk and it is safe to do so, examine them. Run your hands over their skin to find any hidden swelling or bumps as well as any hot spots. Notice any scratches or blood, too. Look under their belly, down their legs, and under their tail for signs of trauma.

You can also use their natural movement to determine if they are experiencing pain. Walk them forward, turn them in each direction, and look for any issues in the way they move. A horse who is colicking, for example, may walk with short, uneven strides as the pain in its belly gets worse. A horse with a sore back may drag their hind legs. A horse with a broken tooth may fling their head around when you apply pressure to the halter and lead rope.

Sometimes the source of pain is obvious and easily treatable. An obvious cut or minor flesh wound can be cleaned and treated. Minor bumps and bruises can be cold-hosed, slathered in a poultice, and relieved with a bit of stall rest.

However, most pain issues aren't immediately recognizable. One common area in which horses experience pain is their spine. The entire length of a horse's spine, from the top of its head to the tip of its tail, can come out of alignment, bruise, twist, and strain. Most of the time, horses experience back pain for the same reasons we do– tension, a little extra-long workout, or taking a weird step are some of the most frequent reasons behind equine back pain. Just like us, a horse can move the wrong way and tweak its back.

And, just like us, horses can benefit from some of the things we do to deal with back pain. Equine chiropractic and massage services are very popular among horses who have high-demand jobs. As a lesson horse, my little mare, Belle, enjoys a chiropractic session each month to help relieve the tension that builds in her jaw, neck, and hips from her frequent workouts. There are also liniments available that help relieve equine pain, just like a lidocaine patch for humans. Careful warm-up and cool-down each time you and your horse work, regular vet work, and a knowledgeable farrier can also help mitigate back pain in your equine companion.

Signs that your horse might be trying to tell you all about their aching back include:

- Not wanting to be caught when it's time to work

- Acting up when being groomed

- Snapping or pinning their ears when being tacked up

- Refusal to go forward under saddle

- A shorter stride

- Picking up the wrong lead in the canter/lope

- Bucking

When you think about it, it makes sense. We don't want to do a whole lot when our backs hurt, either. If your horse is suddenly acting like having a job is a "very big deal," or isn't moving quite the same as they have in the past, they might be trying to explain that they have a valid reason for their unwillingness.

The treatment for a sore back depends on the severity, cause, and each horse's individual needs, so if you feel your horse is truly in pain, consult with your veterinarian for some ideas for helping your horse feel better quickly.

At the same time, not all pain is back pain. Horses also display similar reactions when they have ulcers. Like humans, horses can develop gastric ulcers. Unlike humans, they are not caused by spicy foods or that late-night slices of pizza. Horses constantly secrete stomach acid, as they're physically designed to move around all day, grazing. Horses kept on smaller pastures or in stalls for long periods don't get to roam around finding new and delicious things to eat. Even if you keep hay and pasture in front of them around the clock, human-made grain feed includes fatty acids that horses' guts don't encounter in nature, which can contribute to ulcers. Furthermore, horses who are in heavy work often develop ulcers due to the rapid cycling of blood through the stomach and body, which can result in a faster metabolism.

In many cases, ulcers can be relieved with dietary changes, but this is not always the case. If you suspect your horse may have ulcers, it's a good idea to contact your veterinarian before making any changes yourself. Making quick changes in a horse's diet can often lead to colic– a sudden impaction of the horse's gut that can lead to serious medical complications– so I strongly recommend consulting with a professional for recommendations.

Mouth pain is another common reason for a major shift in a horse's attitude toward work and human interaction in general. If you notice your horse has suddenly become head shy—meaning they won't let you put their halter or fly mask on or touch their face—and has a strong opinion about being led around on a lead rope, they might be trying to tell you about pain in their mouth.

Horses' mouths are fascinating—to me, at least. Behind their large, flexible lips, they have sharp teeth in the front to tear at plants and large flat molars in the back that grind those plants to a digestible pulp. In between these teeth, they have a small gap, which is where we put the bit.

The shape, size, and function of a horse's teeth make sense when you take into account that they're supposed to be grazing all day. In fact, horse teeth continue to erupt from the gumline at a rate of 3-4 millimeters each year to accommodate for the natural wear and tear of constantly eating roughage.

Our domesticated horses don't spend all day eating roughage in a sense that their ancestors would recognize. Our modern horses get– or at least think they deserve– silky smooth second-cutting hay and pasture that has typically been cultivated to eliminate plants that are toxic to horses.

As a result, their teeth occasionally erupt faster than they wear down. Horses truly get "long in the tooth" when this happens. That's why many vets recommend having your horse's teeth floated—or filed down—by a professional equine dentist at least once a year.

If left alone, most horses who get long in the tooth experience serious sensitivity in their mouths. The rough edges of their teeth can cut up the inside of their mouths and tongues, which is even more uncomfortable. Occasionally, a wound caused by a long tooth will ulcerate, which can then cause an abscess on the inside or outside of a horse's mouth.

Horses can also be clumsy, like we are, and can bite their tongues or cheeks. They can chip or crack their teeth. They can accidentally hit their heads on something and end up with a puffy, swollen injury on their face. If your horse is acting strange about their face out of nowhere, you might want to check them for a wound before contacting your equine dentist.

A Word about Incorrect Tack

A wise horseperson once told me, "Improper tack is the reason behind 98% of the things wrong in your life, from your horse's attitude to his performance to your back pain and oily T-zone." The part about skincare is debatable, but the rest is very true.

Many of us are guilty of having some piece of clothing or shoes that doesn't particularly feel great, yet we can't let go of it, either because it looks great, we can't afford to replace it, or it just doesn't feel right to get rid of. Don't worry—I'm not here to judge. I confess to having a pair of ballet flats that I keep only because I wear them infrequently enough to forget how much I hate wearing them.

Every time you wear this particular item, you regret it. You get blisters, there's chafing, you're constantly fiddling with it in an attempt to make it comfortable, and the minute you can remove the offending item, you practically celebrate.

What if this were your horse's saddle, bit, or bridle? Imagine forcing your sweet equine friend to put on that uncomfortable piece of clothing and then perform to the best of their ability. They don't have thumbs to adjust what's on their body. Instead, they may resort to acting "naughty," prancing in place, throwing their head around, hopping and bucking, and pulling the reins out of your hand when you try to give them direction.

In most cases, we are completely unaware of an issue with how our tack fits until our horse is about at its wit's end trying to tell us about it. One summer, I found myself losing patience with Belle. She was acting moody under saddle, so I had the chiropractor and the dentist out. I treated her for ulcers. I had the farrier rebalance her hooves. After all that, it turned out she didn't like the saddle and bit we were using. As the kids who had been riding her gained more and more experience, she'd gained more and more muscle, to the point where her saddle was now pinching her in several spots across her back. And, as the kids became more confident riding her in a certain contact, her mouth became more sensitive to their hands, so changing to a bit that was more accommodating to the shape and size of her mouth and tongue made her much happier.

Unfortunately for us humans, good riding equipment is *expensive*. Tack swaps, online sales forums, and consignment shops are incredibly helpful in offsetting the cost of saddles, bridles, bits, girths, reins, stirrup leathers, and more, but many of us—myself included—have trouble coughing up a handful of hundred dollar bills every time our horse changes shape or decides they'd like something different. I strongly recommend looking into local saddle fitters to help you evaluate your saddle fit. They can often help reshape your saddle, offer tips on what type of padding can help, and make recommendations for brands and styles of saddles that might fit you and your horse.

There are many mysterious ways in which horses can experience pain and try to tell us about it. As many wise and weary horseperson have discovered, these gorgeous creatures could manage to damage themselves in a bubble, if they were so inclined. Therefore, if your horse starts acting strangely out of nowhere, it is a very good idea to check for pain. From hooves to ears and nose to tail, there are plenty of secret places your horse might be hiding something ouchy.

Boredom

A few pages ago, I asked you to compare living in a stall as a horse to what you might experience living in a bathroom as a human. I didn't mention that, while you're confined in this small space, you don't have your phone, books, or television with you. You might get some music, as many barns leave radios on to scare away local wildlife, but you don't get to choose the station. Depending on your attention span and overall comfort with the close quarters, you might last a few days or a few minutes before you become exceedingly bored.

Horse brains are different from human brains in many ways. In many cases, a stalled horse can be entertained for hours just watching things happen in the barn aisleway or outside the barn, if they're lucky enough to have a window. I refer to Red as "the snooping neighbor" because he is extremely interested in everything that is going on both in and outside the barn. He actually moves his hay to the side of his stall with a window so he can eat his meals while watching cars, animals, and humans go by. I have to clean up the hay he drops outside once a week, and I roll my eyes as he flirts with the lesson kids in an attempt to get treats just for being cute and charming.

Red is a Thoroughbred, and he was bred to be a racehorse. That means he's genetically designed to be a top-level athlete. In reality, he's not incredibly athletic. He enjoys schooling First Level Dressage, and he's game to jump things under two feet in height, but he's not trying to exert too much effort. As a result, his instincts say "go, go, go" while his body says, "Nah, let's watch the garbage truck come by."

Eventually, this disparity catches up with him, and his ancestors whisper encouraging words to him about galloping like the wind and bucking and running like a fool. On most days, Red loves snuggling and playing with the children who come for their lessons. When his boredom kicks in, you'd think he was a former Triple Crown champion.

His head shoots up and his ears prick forward at every little noise. He is on high alert, searching for things that are moving, making sounds, or could potentially be a threat. He trots in circles in his stall. He kicks the walls and squeals like a toddler who has his heart set on a particular toy.

When he gets like this, I need to be careful when handling him. He has excellent manners on a normal day, but when boredom settles in, he doesn't care if you have specific instructions—he just wants to GO!

In Red's case, the issue is frequently resolved with some turnout in the pasture or a good 10-15 minutes of lunging in the arena. He has a tantrum, runs as fast as he can, snorts, bucks into the air, rolls around in the mud, darts this way and that...and then it's done, and my impressively placid former racehorse is back in all his mild glory.

From their teeth and their guts to their emotional processing systems, horses are meant to be constantly on the move, finding food and avoiding danger. Most of them are perfectly content with a few hours of distraction, whether that's riding, training, pasture time, or human interaction like grooming, groundwork, and plain old hanging out together.

However, there are times when a horse needs mental stimulation while releasing energy. If your normally placid horse is starting to:

- Act bossy or like they have never been polite in their life

- Take up bad habits in their stall (more on that in the next section!)

- Bolt, kick, or rear when you try to handle them

- Escape his pasture or stall

- Fight with other horses

- Remind you of a small child on the brink of a tantrum

Then chances are good that they are experiencing boredom on a level they do not feel they can live with.

Boredom can be natural whenever things change in a horse's life. If you just bought a horse who was turned out all day and night, and expect them to stay inside all night, they might act out at the prospect of being "locked up." If you've changed turnout times or locations, the feeding schedule, or the training schedule, your horse might experience boredom. Some, like Red, get really upset when the days turn colder and shorter in the winter because they don't get to hang their head out the window and stare at things for a blissful fifteen hours a day!

The biggest downside to equine boredom is that it often results in inappropriate behavior. It may seem like your horse simply throws logic to the wayside and turns into an actual beast; in fact, this is actually pretty accurate. Nearly all of us have experienced moments of soul-crushing boredom, but as humans, we could find ways to release that mental and physical energy.

Some horses enjoy stall toys as a way to end their boredom. Some enjoy a change of scenery, like switching to the stall across the aisle because it provides a totally new perspective on things. Others actually require constant work and turn out to keep them happy. In some cases, changing your feeding program can mellow a horse out—sweet feed and rich hay can occasionally cause horses to act as if they've feasted on sugar and caffeine.

It's also possible for horses to get tired of working on the same thing over and over again. Like us, they can get frustrated or flustered when they aren't able to do things right the first time. Most experts recommend changing things up in your horse's exercise regimen to keep their mind fresh and interested. That doesn't mean you have to go out of your way to think up new and exciting things to do with your horse, but if you've been working on walk-canter transitions for more than a few sessions, perhaps it's time to let your equine buddy trot their feelings out to get a fresh perspective on the task at hand.

Horses are not machines. They observe the world around them in keen detail, constantly scanning their environment for potential threats. Though we can help them understand what is and isn't actually dangerous, we can't entirely shut down the way they see and process the information presented to them. Furthermore, if we remove all potential stimulation and entertainment by confining them to a stall all day and night, their brains are going to find new and exciting ways to distract themselves—things humans can't even fathom. Common activities bored equines turn to include using their mouths, feet, and bodies to destroy things. Others enjoy finding creative ways to solve problems and turn into escape artists.

Your horse will attempt to tell you how bored they are, but most of us don't entirely appreciate the delivery of this message. Observe your horse to get a feel for what their "normal" daily behavior is like, and when you find them acting particularly obstreperous, first consider pain, then ask yourself if your fluffy friend could potentially be bored. Many times, with a little guided play time to get the bucks out, a bored horse will calm down quickly. If not, you may wish to work with a trainer or veterinarian to determine the cause of your horse's boredom, and what you can do to help them find a little more serenity in their lives.

Poor or No Training

I hate to use the term "poor" when referring to training because I would love to believe that somewhere, deep down, every person is trying to do their best to teach their horses about their environment and learn to communicate with them. However, after over a decade of working with owner-surrendered, kill auction-bound, and otherwise rescued horses, I know that this is not the case.

It is possible to find a horse that has lived well into its teen years without having been handled by humans besides being thrown into a field and forgotten about. While we often expect horses in this category to be thin with torn-up mouths and overgrown hooves, this isn't always the case. After all, they're living the life that was intended for them, grazing and moving all day, every day. These semi-feral horses often have loads of parasites and skin conditions, but as long as they had adequate forage and room to move around for their entire lives, this isn't always a sad story.

Those are the exceptions, however. All too often, we find semi-feral horses in barns filled to the brim with manure, hooves overgrown into what we call an "elf shoe," and having difficulty breathing and moving due to the lack of fresh air and space. They may be too thin or too large, depending on what they've had for feed.

Creating a soft landing for these horses can be difficult because they don't understand how to be handled. Much of the time, rescuers and animal welfare folks need to rely on a horse's survival instincts to convince it to get on the trailer to safety. Unloading them at their new facility is generally a matter of creating chutes and corrals. But then comes the point where they need to be evaluated by a veterinarian and treated by a farrier. As you can imagine, all of these things are absolutely terrifying for a horse who has never been touched by a human being before.

Typically, horses who have been surrendered, rescued, or pulled from a kill pen are physically rehabilitated and adopted out to a new home, where they'll be loved and treated kindly for the rest of their lives. Many adoption fees are pretty low, compared to the price of a well-trained horse with miles and miles of experience. As a result, adopting an untrained horse is often an attractive option for folks who are new to horses and don't want to spend a lot of money on their first beast.

There's an old adage that, "a free horse costs more than an expensive horse," and in my experience, this is generally true. I paid $10 for Red. I also spent about $5,000 in vet bills, x-rays, medication, supplements, supplies, feed, and dentistry within the first year of having him... and about $300 of that was a saddle that would fit his strangely narrow conformation.

You might be thinking, "Well sure, but that's just one horse," and I absolutely agree. There have been many rescues that didn't require an investment of money, but rather time and skill. One way or another, the less money and effort you spend purchasing the horse, the more money and effort you'll have to invest in helping them become your ideal equine partner.

No training, however, is often easier to work with than poor training. A horse who knows nothing isn't aware of complicated evasion tactics, nor can it anticipate what you might ask them to do. In many cases, they're running off of pure instinct, and if they've never known harsh treatment, they might be more interested in what humans have to say.

A horse who has been poorly trained may be unpredictable, angry, and unwilling to change its mind about the hospitality of humans. I once worked with a rescued pony named Dora. Despite being quite small and compact, she had a big, fluid trot, acted like a dream partner on the trails, and thought it was pretty fun to jump over a log here or there. However, she knew nothing about arena work. In fact, when ridden in an arena, she would panic and slam her body into the fence in an attempt to lose me. I never knew when this was going to happen, exactly. Generally, it had to do with asking her to try something different, but sometimes we'd be in the middle of walking around on a loose rein and she'd try it.

Dora had been sold to a woman as a children's riding pony for $500, but no one mentioned that she should only be ridden on the trail. The price was right at the time for a 4H horse, but the horse was definitely not right for 4H! My buddies at that particular rescue worked with her diligently for many months before we felt she was safe enough to find a new home, and I was thrilled when she became a children's field hunter.

Was Dora broke to ride? Sure... but only in certain conditions. She was trained, but not in the way anyone expected. A horse does not necessarily need to know how to work politely in a ring, as long as that horse isn't going to a home that needs them to work politely in a ring.

A horse who is sold as a child's 4H horse, however, needs to know a lot of things about politeness.

A similar example was a horse who I came to know through the rescue as a surrender. She was in fantastic health and had recently retired from a career as a barrel racer. She kept coming up lame for competitions, so her owner decided to rehome her because when she wasn't racing, she was sound. This is common in performance horses who have experienced an injury or simply have joint issues after years of very hard work. We determined she wasn't in any active pain, then decided to see how she was under saddle.

My first time attempting to ride her lasted about four seconds. As I put my foot in the stirrup, she bolted off. I was left standing on the mounting block with one leg raised, wondering what was going on. I brought her back, and the same thing happened over and over. It turns out, her previous trainer had taught her to start running the minute he put his foot in the stirrup because he would get on her right outside the pen. That way, he didn't have to worry about getting her into a gallop before they hit the timer in competitions.

As you can imagine, this particular trait is pretty undesirable in any other riding situation. Once I knew the situation, I was able to work with her to help her understand how to stand still for mounting. The process took a little over a month of consistent, calm discussion. She was fantastic under saddle, otherwise, but it took her a while to appreciate that there were other options available to her. She went on to become a dressage pony with plenty of 4H ribbons to her credit.

When we bring a horse into our lives, we aren't always aware of what they know and don't know. "Experience" is not the same as "training." Furthermore, even a well-trained horse can be a handful, depending on their temperament. We often look at price tags when we're horse shopping, and forget about the part where we actually need to be able to work with this horse regularly. Given my choice between a $10 Red and a $100,000 well-trained horse, I would choose Red every time, but that's because I knew a thing or two about how racehorses were trained and could work with a baby racehorse who had been left out to pasture. Had I not had this information beforehand, I would've been completely terrified of how he behaves when he's bored, or how little he knew about steering and straightness under saddle.

Bringing home a horse not only means providing them a safe, sustainable place to physically thrive but also offering them a partnership where they can trust and understand what's going on. Horses with poor or no training may not be on the same page with you at first, but with time, patience, and plenty of consistent work, they certainly can be. Therefore, if you have a horse who seems to have a Jekyll/Hyde personality, take a step back and consider where it came from and what you know about its past. They may be frightened, angry, or doing the best they can with what they know.

Does a lack of training excuse bad behavior? No, but it does give you an idea of where your horse is coming from when they react poorly to what you consider calm and clear commands. I consider it a starting place for good things to come and recognize that the path might not be as straightforward as I imagined.

Prior Abuse or Trauma

In some cases, there is a very thick, blurry line between abuse or trauma and poor training. That's because horses, like humans, experience similar things in different ways. Some horses, like Red, have a pretty "whatever" attitude to most things. Other horses, like Belle, need to have a safe and therapeutic environment with extremely patient hands until they learn how to trust themselves and the people with whom they interact.

Belle is very well-bred and exceptionally well-trained. However, Belle was in a situation that she didn't like very much for several months, then bounced around between homes for a few months after that. As a result, the little mare that unloaded from the trailer at her current home with me was skittish, defiant, angry, and frightened. When anyone would walk into her stall, she would plaster herself against the back wall, pinning her ears back and baring her teeth to let everyone know there were to be no shenanigans in her presence. When working with her, she would walk, trot, and canter easily on command, but she was quite robotic about it. Her head froze into place, and there was something frantic about the way she acted. Furthermore, she had a relentless twitch in her left eye whenever she was interacting with humans.

I can only speculate as to what she had experienced, being familiar with some of the places she had been on her journey. So, my trainer and I decided to contact the equine behaviorist she had worked with for many years. A very kind, quiet soul, this particular gentleman introduced himself to Belle, groomed her and talked to her, then took her into the arena using his own halter and lunge line to see what she would do.

At his first request to move away from him, she exploded into a cloud of equine fury. She reared, bolted, and refused to move, rotating between the three actions as she saw fit. The behaviorist then simply asked her to walk forward. After 20 minutes, she took 2 steps, and he rewarded her with positive attention, treats, and letting her stop for the day. He never raised his voice, struck her, or used so much as aggressive body language. Yet Belle clearly felt threatened.

He warned me that she is clearly processing some kind of trauma, and to just walk her around on the lead rope as much as possible until she relaxed about having someone ask her to move her feet. And that's exactly what I did.

Belle had been trained in Showmanship, which is a type of equestrian competition where horses and handlers are judged in hand. That means no riding– the horse is led by the handler through a pattern of movements, including walk, trot, halt, and pivots. I had only dabbled in Showmanship under a previous trainer, so I unlocked a few memories in hopes that it would help unlock Belle's resistance. Each day, we'd head into the arena and walk in a line, trot a few steps, back up a few steps, and do 90-degree turns towards and away from me.

At first, she resisted completely. Then she relented in that robotically obedient way. One day, I noticed her neck wasn't as stiff. Eventually, her eye stopped twitching. Now we can do these moves without a lead rope; in fact, I frequently warm her up for a day of lessons by putting her through these exercises. As I do so, I pay attention to how relaxed or tense she is, where her ears are, and how she's moving. If her ears are pricked and her neck raised and tense, I know she needs to work through some feelings before anyone rides her. If she seems pretty bored, I know she's ready to move on to something more thought-provoking.

I tell you this story not because I think it will solve all of your problems, but because it's just one of many similar experiences I've had working with horses. I can't even say "rescue" horses in particular because there are some very well-trained, intelligent horses who have– for some reason or another– some strange trauma blip in their training.

Sometimes, this has absolutely nothing to do with humans. Red doesn't like light grey horses. Once upon a time, he was in a herd with two grey horses who used to chase him around the pasture. On one particular chase, Red ended up getting caught in the fence and sliced up his leg trying to free himself. To this day, he is aggressive towards light grey horses in the pasture.

Horses can experience trauma anywhere. Many times, it's their own doing. A horse who injures itself evading a human request may do everything in its power to avoid things that remind them of that event. A horse who got tangled in a hose might bolt every time it sees a hose. They may react strongly to certain types of fences or objects they associate with "the bad thing that happened." With trust and patience, they can come to understand that not everything is out to get them, but it's not a quick process.

Unless you have known your horse from the moment it opened its eyes, it's usually hard to tell what trauma a horse carries until it's actively triggered. Furthermore, trauma reactions can vary greatly. Some horses go into robot mode like Belle, others choose an option from the "fight, flight, or freeze" suite of instincts. If your horse has an unexpected, seemingly uncontrolled reaction to a situation, for no apparent reason, it could be holding on to some trauma.

When this happens, it's a sign that it's time to have a nice, calm, quiet discussion with the horse in a place where it's unlikely to hurt itself. Depending on how traumatized the horse actually is, this may be dangerous for an inexperienced person, so when in doubt, call a professional.

While a horse can get over the mental and emotional scars of trauma and abuse, there are some instances in which the horse will not accept that things will be ok. You may need to make some concessions to accommodate your horse's fears. That may be as low-tech as rearranging the turnout schedule, to as extreme as working with your vet to administer tranquilizers as needed for certain situations. There are feed supplements that work as calming agents, as well. Regardless of which option works best for you and your horse, patience is key when working with a horse who has been traumatized. Give them a chance to work through their fears, and always make safety a priority for everyone involved.

Once I Know, What Should I Do?

If your horse's behavioral issues stem from a physical problem, your vet, farrier, and/or dentist should be able to provide you with some guidelines for helping your horse become more comfortable. In many cases, pain issues can be relieved with relatively simple means, such as changing how the hooves are balanced, buying a new saddle pad to help your saddle conform to your horse's back better, or trying a regular supplement or medication. Of course, there are exceptions to this, so you'll need to decide what is feasible for you and the horse, including your budget and time constraints.

Boredom issues can be tricky since you might already be short on time and space. However, you might look into equine enrichment toys, or consider leasing or free-leasing them to someone who can spend more time with them. You can pay a trainer to work with them during your busy periods, so they can continue to learn and grow when you need to focus on other things. You might consider getting them a companion like a goat or mini pony, if your budget permits.

Training issues and trauma can be tricky, especially if you don't know the specific parameters of what your horse does and doesn't know and what they will and won't react to. I recommend calling in a professional, even if you are pretty sure you know what you're doing. A second set of eyes can be very helpful when noticing highly nuanced things about body language. I used to think that Red's attitude problem on the lunge line was naughtiness until my friend pointed out that it was only going in one direction, in just one spot in the arena. The hard footing in that spot was causing him pain, and one hoof supplement and a call to the farrier later, he lost complete interest in that spot.

And without a doubt, some horses are naturally more ornery than others. There are horses with defiant streaks, and in many cases, this attitude only perpetuates or gets worse as they go from owner to owner who can't—or won't—deal with it. But, if you look at it from the horse's point of view, this is actually a training gap. If you don't deal with a horse's behavioral issues or challenges, they aren't going to just get better on their own.

It is ok to admit that you cannot work with your horse. Perhaps you can't afford the treatment that will help them feel physically capable of doing what you ask of them. Many horses are described as "pasture sound," which means they are not physically able to be ridden or worked, but they're otherwise healthy. You may also hear the terms "lawn ornaments" or "pasture puffs" when referring to these beasts.

If you aren't able to afford treatment, you may not have the budget for a pasture sound-only horse, either. It may not be feasible for you to build your horse a 20-acre pasture with a carefully cultivated herd of buddies. You may not have the physical ability or training experience to deal with your horse's training and trauma issues on your own. All of these are legitimate reasons to reconsider your relationship with your horse.

Not every horse and human will have a magical connection. There have been several horses with whom I've had a "politeness is required" working relationship. Many horses have disregarded me with a cold side-eye, and I was experienced enough to return the favor.

Once you've discovered the cause of your horse's naughtiness, I encourage you to be honest with yourself about whether or not this is something you can handle, much less handle on your own. Being intimidated or outmatched is perfectly okay, as long as you're honest with yourself and your horse.

You're allowed to request assistance, ask questions, and get second or third opinions as you try to get down to the source of what is causing your horse to act this way. Most of the time, this isn't the end of a partnership—though if it is, make sure you do the most responsible thing for your horse. Rehoming your horse to a responsible person with more experience or resources at their disposal is a great choice. You may also have to have a terrible but frank conversation with your vet about quality of life and make some equally awful decisions. However, I'm an advocate of acting in the best interest of the horse, regardless of how challenging or emotionally brutal that decision may be.

So that we don't end on that depressing note, I'd like to add that there are many happy stories out there. As you read, my two horses have not had a charmed life, but they are beloved by the individuals they've met along the way. I have very happy memories of Red cuddling with my roommate after she'd had a bad day at work, and Belle standing stock-still while a very frightened child fought back tears because she wanted to pat a pony so badly.

My trainer and I like to joke that, "there are a few redeeming factors about horses," and one of those is their honesty. When a horse acts inappropriately, chances are very high that they are trying to tell you something important. Sure, they may be having a naughty moment, but if you notice a pattern in their behavior, or it comes out of nowhere, it might be time to ask yourself whether pain, boredom, training, or trauma could be at fault.

When your horse is doing something particularly naughty, out of character, or dangerous, start the path to ending this behavior by asking these four questions:

- Could my horse be in pain?

- Are they bored and need to release some energy?

- Is this how they were trained?

- Could there be trauma behind this situation?

In the heat of the moment, when everything is chaotic and everyone is upset, it may be hard to remember that your horse is trying to tell you there is a problem that needs your immediate attention. However, once everyone has had a chance to calm down and reflect, you may find that there was a reasonable explanation behind why your horse reacted as it did.

Make note of any patterns or warning signs that your horse may be used to get your attention. Pinned ears are the first line of communication for many horses, so make sure you're observing your horse's ear and body language. I've included some links in the Resources section to help you start translating Horse to Human.

If your horse is not in pain, not bored, has sterling training, and has never had a bad day in their life, you're allowed to be confused about bad behavior. I would be, too.

Chapter Three

Bad Barn Habits and How to Deal with Them

So how does equine naughtiness manifest itself? Many ways! Most people are bothered by horses that:

- Exhibit bad barn habits

- Are hard to handle

- Act like a fool under saddle

I'm going to skip the last one for this discussion because there are nearly infinite reasons why a horse may have poor manners under saddle, from the aforementioned poor-fitting tack and oily t-zone to the position of your left elbow on the second full moon of the year. All horses and riders are different, not only from each other but from themselves, on any given day. Both a horse and a human bring all of their emotions and experiences to the arena, so there can be so many different reasons for a horse to act up. Always run through the checklist of pain, boredom, training, and trauma when your horse misbehaves during work sessions, and look for patterns to help you narrow down possible causes.

"Barn habits" is the umbrella term for what horses do and how they act in their home. Horses who don't live in a stall can still have bad "barn habits," as this refers more to the constraints of domestication rather than the architectural style of their home. You may also hear terms like "stall or stable vice" or "troubled keeper" when referring to these behaviors and horses.

Horses may be genetically predisposed to disliking captivity, but that doesn't mean they should get away with bad behavior. It can be very easy for a horse to injure themselves in a stall or on a fence or gate. There are often physical complications from these types of habits, as well.

You may be surprised to learn that horses are creative... in the same way, we might refer to a chaotic toddler as "creative." There are many things they can do in their stall, paddock, or pasture that will drive you up the wall. Some of the most common bad habits include cribbing, chewing, weaving, stall walking, kicking, and my personal least favorite—biting. Let's take a look at each of these habits to get an idea of why your horse does this, and what can be done to prevent it.

Cribbing and Chewing

Cribbing and chewing can be such severe issues with some horses that boarding barns will not allow horses who commit these sins to stay on the premises. There are many reasons why cribbing and chewing are terrible habits that must be discouraged, but from the point of view of the property owner, it's downright destructive.

"Cribbing" is an equine activity in which they firmly grasp an object with their teeth, such as a bucket, Dutch door ledge, fence line, tree branch, friend's neck, or enemy's tail, stretch their necks, and loudly suck in air while stretching backward.

This is "bad" for several reasons:

1. It's annoying. Also known as "windsucking," horses make a loud, repetitive "HRRRUNNNK!" noise as the air rapidly passes through their windpipe.

2. It is destructive. While cribbing doesn't always include chewing, the constant strain on your walls, latches, equipment, or horse's relationships can be damaging. I'm not joking about cribbing on other horses, either– I've seen several serial cribbers latch onto another horse during mutual grooming or playtime to get a good gulp.

3. It has been linked to health issues such as gastric ulcers and colic. The action has been known to irritate a horse's esophagus, as well as prematurely wear down their front teeth.

4. It's an addiction. Researchers have found that cribbing contributes to the release of endorphins. Just as in humans, a surge of endorphins feels good for horses. Unless cribbing is prevented, a horse simply will not stop.

Many experts believe that horses crib due to genetics, boredom, trauma, or a combination of all three. Unfortunately, it's not entirely known why some horses crib and others do not. Historically, we thought that cribbing was a bad habit horse picked up from each other, like rebellious teenagers teaching each other how to smoke. Experts now feel that's not correct, and a more likely explanation for several horses picking up the same terrible habit is due to environmental stressors.

Still, very little is understood about this instinct, though researchers have studied cribbing behavior in horses both born in captivity and formerly feral horses living in captivity, which indicates that it's inherent to a horse's instinct. Perhaps even *Eohippus* was prone to cribbing on low-hanging branches!

There are many strategies employed to dissuade horses from cribbing, and predictably, not all of them work on all horses. For many years, the gold standard for ending cribbing has been smearing a foul-smelling or foul-tasting substance on any potential cribbing surfaces. Hot sauce and purpose-made substances like Farnam's No-Chew are popular choices, with plenty of home brews in between.

However, there are plenty of stable owners who don't cherish the idea of hot sauce dripping from their walls. As a result, cribbing straps and muzzles have become a popular way to curb the cribbers. A cribbing strap– also called a cribbing collar– fits around the horse's neck, right behind the ears and jaws. When the horse is holding their head in a neutral position, or stretching down to graze, the collar is loose. When the horse pulls his neck back to suck in a big breath of air, the collar squeezes on his throat to prevent him from getting the air in quickly. Some straps do this with a nutcracker-type mechanism that pushes on both sides of the neck, while others have a thick center wedge that prevents the horse from getting into the cribbing position.

There are some controversial approaches to ending cribbing. Horses can have neck muscles surgically removed or modified to prevent cribbing. Oral implants such as rings pierced through the gums have also been found effective in ending the behavior. As you can imagine, there are significant risks with either procedure, as well as mixed opinions, anecdotes, and data regarding its success.

Cribbing and chewing often go hand-in-hand, but they can be mutually exclusive. Cribbing seems to be more of a pleasure-seeking or stress-relieving behavior while chewing is often more of an oral fixation.

As the name implies, "chewing" refers to when a horse starts gnawing on something it shouldn't. Typically, this substance is wood, so you may hear this behavior referred to as "wood chewing" as well. From experience, I can tell you that chewing is not always limited to wood, but it's definitely most noticeable and destructive on these surfaces.

Unlike cribbing, we know exactly why horses chew on things. Bored horses will chew, as well as those who are experiencing a nutritional deficit. Imagine, if you will, being genetically predisposed to wanting to chew and digest stuff all day. However, you're hanging out in this single room all day, and your access to roughage is somewhat limited. You might find something else to gnaw on to subdue the cravings. So, a horse will chomp down on a fence post, the side of a stall, a Dutch door, a ledge, a tree, or any solid object and turn it into a snack.

I have seen horses chewing on non-wooden surfaces, such as metal or fiberglass stall walls. I have also known horses who chewed on halters, blankets, bridles, reins, or anything they could drag into their stall and destroy. Same bad habit; different media.

Besides being a destructive behavior, chewing is primarily a concern because of what the horse may potentially ingest. Wood splinters aren't exactly digestible, and while horses need a significant amount of fiber to stay healthy, they don't need the kind that can poke holes in their intestinal lining. They don't need any foreign objects in their tummies. Horses have 70 combined feet of intestines floating inside them, and they are physically unable to vomit. Anything that enters their digestive tracts without prior approval is a liability. Colic is scary and unpleasant at best, and fatal at worst. Therefore, it's a very good idea to mitigate risk by limiting what your horse swallows.

Injuries to the mouth, such as cuts to the lips, gums, tongue, and cheek can also result from chewing. Furthermore, depending on what your horse is chewing, they could inadvertently cause a bigger issue. Jagged edges inside the stall can be hazardous for anyone who enters.

Chewing through a fence can lead to herd members making a run for it, or ending up in a location that isn't safe for them. Years ago, Red and I boarded at a barn where his next-door neighbor was a chewer. The stalls had flat fiberglass and steel panels, with bars located too high for Red to successfully latch onto them to the crib.

Even better, each stall had its own dirt paddock. No grass grew there, but they had plenty of room to wander in and out of their stalls throughout the day and night. On top of that, each paddock opened out on a fenced-in pasture several acres in size, with trees to snooze under, mud pits to wallow in, and interesting views of the woods and pond. By all means, this was the textbook definition of "domesticated horse heaven."

And yet, I was still only somewhat surprised when I opened the barn door to find both horses standing in Red's stall. The chewer had managed to whittle his way through the fence that separated the two of them, so they had a semi-amicable slumber party at Red's place. Remember what I said earlier about bachelor horses and ever-changing herd dynamics? In this case, there were mercifully just a few scratches and bumps. Once the fence was repaired and they were returned to their normal "open door" turnout, it was as if nothing had happened.

For the most part, it's not a matter of stopping the behavior but minimizing risk. In many cases, I've seen chewing behavior "cured" by giving the horse as much hay and/or turnout as they can handle, even though that didn't work for Red's buddy. In several instances, a dietary change helped the horse get the nutrients they were craving and stopped its instinctual need to chew. However, some horses are in it for the long haul, like cribbers.

Grazing muzzles are a popular option for those hoping to stop their horse from chewing a hole in the fence or stall door. These muzzles have strategically placed metal bars that allow horses to eat and drink normally, but prevent them from stretching out their lips to accommodate a thicker, more solid piece of wood. The foul-tasting and smelling substances used to dissuade cribbers also come into play for chewers, as well. Adding stall toys, giving your horse a stall with an interesting view, and increasing their workload are also popular and effective options for preventing chewing.

In an ideal world, our horses would have custom-built dwellings and acreage that suit all of their needs—physically and mentally. We'd be able to work with them in a meaningful way every time they wanted to work, and they'd never experience a moment of stress. But even in "domesticated horse heaven," our noble beasts can still experience boredom and stress.

I know many people—including myself—blame themselves for their horses' bad habits, especially when boredom is the culprit. However, we have to acknowledge areas where we can improve and those in which we are doing the best we can. Yes, it would be great if we could hang out with our horses every second of every day, but most of us have other commitments. Family, school, work, friends, and even taking care of our own health and wellness can get in the way of our planned equine activities. You are not a bad horse person if your horse is a cribber or a chewer. Some humans smoke cigarettes and chew their fingernails. Habits are hard to quit, especially if those habits are hard-wired into your instinct.

That being said, it is the duty of the responsible horse person to help their horse with this behavior. This may be by providing more enrichment and activity, addressing dietary needs, or using appropriate equipment to reduce the risk associated with this behavior.

On the surface, cribbing and chewing are annoying at best and destructive to your property and pony at worst. But there can be dangers associated with these behaviors, which makes it a good idea to get to the root of the issue and do your best to prevent it from happening.

Weaving and Stall Walking

Weaving and stall walking are both relatively mild vices– but that doesn't make them any less important to understand. Neither weaving nor stall walking is inherently dangerous to the horse or your barn, but they can be troublesome to observe.

"Weaving" is a very specific equine activity that is typically observed only when a horse is stalled, though some horses engage in this type of behavior when tied for long periods, and others will weave when waiting to come in from the field. When weaving, the horse typically stands in place while swaying back and forth, rhythmically shifting its weight from the left front hoof to the right front hoof and back again. Some horses turn this into a full-body boogie, and wave their heads and necks from side to side as they weave.

Horses who weave generally don't have any physical issues, though they can wear out shoes easily and unbalance their hooves. Additionally, they can experience soreness in their shoulders and neck from the constant movement.

Above anything else, weaving is compulsive. The horses who weave can't control their behavior, so you can't really train them to stop doing it. Furthermore, any type of restraint that might stop the behavior would be dangerous for long-term use.

Therefore, instead of stopping weaving, most horse people are tasked with understanding where this behavior comes from so that the horse doesn't feel the need to do it.

Most experts agree that weaving is an indicator of stress. Unfortunately, we don't always know what stresses horses out. Boredom is at the top of the list, of course. Horses who have had a change in living situation—for instance, living mostly outdoors and then mostly indoors—can weave to demonstrate their frustration at not being able to roam all day. Some horses weave to express displeasure at changes in routine, location, or even diet.

Not having enough social interaction has also been linked to weaving. Some horses need to see other horses to feel like everything is ok. This makes sense, as they are herd animals. They want to know what's going on, and whether it's safe to eat or lie down. They can't relax unless they've got the "all-clear" from the herd leader.

Unfortunately, there's not a lot that can be done about weaving, other than providing your horse with lots of distractions, pasture time, and buddies. In many cases, weaving may disappear for a while, only to return when your horse finds something new that troubles him.

The good news is that weaving is rarely dangerous to you or your horse. It's never a bad idea to ask your vet to check out a horse who suddenly starts weaving to make sure they aren't trying to tell you about a new source of pain and to make sure they haven't caused themselves mischief with this behavior.

Stall walking is similar to weaving, in that it is a compulsive behavior. It can be somewhat eerie to observe because horses who stall walk often seem to go into a trance-like state after a few laps. Essentially the equine equivalent of pacing back and forth, stall walking generally involves a horse wandering in circles in its stall repeatedly.

Like weaving, it's not necessarily dangerous, unless your horse is spending a lot of time doing it. Just like an athlete who works out only one side of their body, your horse will have trouble moving in the other direction and may be sore under the saddle more frequently. The wear pattern on their hooves will also reflect this habit, so you may need to call the farrier more frequently.

In my opinion, the worst thing about stall walking is how quickly these horses go through the bedding. There are plenty of horses who are decent housekeepers, putting their manure in specific piles or corners in their stalls. Stall walkers may do this too, but we would never know, because the constant pacing mixes the manure and urine with fresh bedding, blending it all into a wet, stinky mess. You may find yourself cleaning a stall walker's bedding more frequently than any other horse's, which can get expensive and drain your time and energy.

I have enjoyed the company of two stall walkers in my equine career, and we managed the musculoskeletal consequences pretty well with the help of regular exercise and turnout in an "interesting" pasture—that is, an area that isn't flat, is large enough to kick up a good gallop, and has enriching things to look at, like the riding arena, other pastures, and nature.

Making sure your horse has a BFF is also important in managing stall walking. Red gets along with many other horses (as long as they're not grey). In each place he's lived, he has had a best friend who either lives with him or is adjacent to him. In his outdoor herd days, he was friends with an overgrown miniature pony. He also makes a great Uncle figure to weanlings, teaching them the ropes of how the pecking order works until they start to get adolescent urges to be the one in charge.

In his current living space, he and Belle can chat with each other through their outdoor windows, and he can look up and down the barn aisleway to see what his other neighbors are up to. He still churns up his stall daily, but not to the point where it becomes a swamp in mere hours. Years ago, I had a barn owner approach me about keeping Red's stall clean. I had just stripped it and re-bedded it a few hours earlier that day.

There can be some aches and pains associated with weaving and stall walking—especially for the humans who have to clean their stalls constantly. It's never a bad idea to consult your vet when you notice these behaviors, as they can be associated with horses who develop ulcers. But in most cases, your goal is to identify what is stressing your horse out, and what you can do to help them feel less anxious about the situation.

It's impossible to remove a horse's stress entirely, especially since they have such strong instincts that aren't entirely compatible with domestication. However, many horses experience significant relief from compulsive behaviors like weaving and stall walking when an effort is made to understand and mitigate their top consequences. Frequently, these stall vices can be relieved with changes to diet, routine, enrichment toys, and boosting your horse's social life; however, in many cases, you won't be able to completely prevent the behavior in the long run. Still, understanding what makes your horse tick and knowing which of his alarm bells is going off can be incredibly helpful in your overall relationship...and it might save you a wheelbarrow or two of bedding!

Kicking and Pawing

At first, glance, kicking and pawing may not seem to have a lot to do with each other– these behaviors take place on opposing ends of the horse! However, each behavior can have serious consequences, and both can be signs that your horse is trying to reach you about their well-being.

"Kicking" is when a horse shifts their weight to their front legs so it can strike backward with its rear legs. They may use one rear leg to beat out a funky rhythm, or double-barrel kick with both hind legs. Kicking is loud, destructive, dangerous, and a good way to get kicked out of a boarding barn.

Most horse people—myself included—find ourselves automatically programmed to throw a horse a flake of hay if they're doing something naughty in their stall. After all, you just read several scenarios in which the anecdote for the bad behavior included "might need more food." It works for chewers and weavers, so why wouldn't it work for kickers?

It does. It does too well, to the point where horses learn that a kick earns them a flake of hay. Then, before you know it, you have become a kick-activated snack dispenser. Other horses may join in the game because who doesn't love an on-demand treat?

Then there's the damage factor. Experts note that a horse kicks with an average of 2,000 pounds of force per square inch. When that kick connects as it's intended to, bones and boards alike can break. While a confirmed kicker rarely intends to kick with that much force regularly, constantly drumming away at the walls can cause long-term pain issues. A horse's musculoskeletal system is designed to kick on an "as needed" basis, not whenever it's stressed or wants a snack.

Shoulder, neck, back, knee, and hip problems often develop faster and more severely in kickers.

Unfortunately, the only truly confirmed way to "correct" kicking is to change whatever it is about the horse's life that's stressing them out, including their feeding program, turnout schedule, who they hang out with, or how often they work, and what type of exercise they get each time. Even then, horses who have discovered the joy of kicking will often give an excited whack or twelve to the wall if you're late with dinner.

"Pawing" happens at the other end. When I was a child, a teacher tried to explain to me that hooved animals couldn't dig holes. And while my delivery was probably immature, I tried to provide the counterpoint that horses most certainly can and do create a variety of divots in the ground with their feet.

In many cases, pawing is very similar to a child making grabby hands at a desired treat or toy. Nearly every horse will use a front hoof to strike at the ground when feeding time arrives, especially once they've heard the rustle of hay or the rattle of grain. In this situation, it's merely an expression of excitement, anticipation, and a smidge of impatience. Horses who deeply enjoy their job even display pawing behavior before work sessions.

Horses have learned how to paw and dig thanks to their ancestors' experiences on snowy plains around the world. Sometimes a horse will need to dig under a layer of snow or ice to reach available nutrition. When a horse is frantically pawing, they are generally trying to tell you that they detect a problem.

If your horse is pawing as an expression of excitement or approval. For some horses, pawing means "Hooray! Good things are happening!" In this case, they'll typically knock it off once they're allowed to do or eat whatever they wanted in the first place. This type of pawing is rarely dangerous, though you may notice the dominant hoof wears down faster due to the repeated striking against the ground.

In other cases, pawing can become problematic. Horses who paw go through a lot of bedding, and can frequently throw their feed and hay out of the stall while they dig. I've also known horses to strategically aim their pawing so their water buckets rattle, which can waste water and cause damage to the bucket. Horses who paw generally fare better with stall mats, as this can prevent them from wearing down the foundation of the barn over time.

Sometimes the cause of pawing is physical. Experts have noted a strong correlation between horses who frequently suffer from ulcers and pawing behavior. It can also be a sign of boredom or stress, as a horse digs to fill what its instincts feel is void.

As a lack of roughage can be a cause of both ulcers and boredom, so many people find that changing their feeding program or adding more turnout can help horses reduce their pawing behavior. However, it's never a bad idea to consult with your veterinarian to eliminate the potential of pain or other physical problems.

Some professionals advocate for devices that limit a horse's range of motion, such as hobbles or chains. The concept isn't bad, since preventing the horse from doing the behavior can eventually discourage them from trying it again. However, if the horse panics, things can go very wrong, very quickly, especially in a tightly confined area like a stall. Determining what is causing this habit and accommodating your horse's needs may take longer, but it has a greater chance of reducing the kicking or pawing without destroying your horse or barn.

Biting

Most horse people would agree that biting is the worst possible stall vice. Nearly every person who has been around horses for decades has a scar or story from a time when a horse got mouthy with them.

Horses have sensitive mouths. Their large upper lip helps them scout out sources of food, select the tastiest pieces of hay, and help them determine whether something in front of their face is safe or not. The many whiskers that surround a horse's lips and nostrils function very much like a cat's whiskers, picking up sensory cues regarding motion and their environment, as well as helping them identify the things in front of them. In many cases, exploring their surroundings with their mouth isn't naughty behavior—they're just trying to check things out.

Horses communicate with each other using their mouths, too. Different types of bites on different parts of the body can mean different things to horses. Two horses who have a warm relationship will use their teeth to lightly nibble at each other, participating in mutual grooming to express their companionship. Your horse may attempt to groom you as you are grooming them, or when they're feeling particularly pleased with what you're doing.

A horse may issue a well-timed warning nip at the side or rear end of another horse to tell them to get out of the way. However, when the teeth come out, there's a problem. Horse teeth are large and meant for grinding roughage. Depending on where you're bitten, a horse bite can break the skin or even bones. When horses bite each other, they don't always break the skin. Mutual grooming involves soft contact, and warning nips are typically aimed to communicate the message without causing damage. If your horse is breaking the skin of another horse, it's a good idea to observe them together closely to see what might be going on.

As we explored earlier, horses frequently re-evaluate the pecking order in the herd. As herd members vie for higher positions in the hierarchy, they'll assert dominance over the lower-ranking members. Frequently, this process looks scarier than it is. There may be squealing, fighting, kicking, and biting, and when two beasts as large as horses start tussling, your own instinct might be to separate them. Generally speaking, this is not a good idea, as the horses will be preoccupied with deciding which one of them is the coolest and not pay attention to your human antics. Instead, keep an eye on them. If they look likely to get tangled in a fence or cause significant damage to each other or their surroundings, use lunge whips or make a racket from the other side of the fence before jumping in to physically separate them.

Another important point regarding herd dynamics is that horses will even display these behaviors in their stall. When someone they don't like walks by, they might lunge at the stall doors and walls with their teeth bared. I like to joke that this is the equine equivalent of insulting each other's mothers, but in some cases, horses will bite at each other and fight through stall walls. This is nearly always solved by separating the horses so they don't have to deal with each other, though sometimes they manage to hash out their differences without inflicting too much damage on themselves and their surroundings.

Horses bite for reasons other than communicating with other horses. The most common reason a horse will start biting with no prior bad behavior is pain. Instead of saying, "Back off, you mere peon," this type of bite is actually meant to communicate, "Don't come near me; I feel awful" or "Stop what you're doing immediately; it hurts."

Belle is very good about telling me when her ulcers are flaring up by snapping at me when I'm tightening her girth before a ride. She's impressively polite about it, but whenever she reacts to tacking up with a few clicks of her teeth, I know it's time to increase her gastric supplement.

I've also experienced horses snapping and nipping when they're body sore, or experiencing a hoof abscess. They may appear vicious, with eye whites showing and ears pinned, but what the horse is really saying is "There's absolutely no way I'm doing what I think you want me to do because I am in pain." A well-trained, well-behaved horse will generally fire off a warning shot to get your attention, then wait to find out what happens next. When you know that your horse is biting because something's wrong, you can go about relieving that pain, which in turn reinforces their trust in you.

But what about rude biters? The horses who just come out of their stalls with teeth bared, who you can't turn your back on for fear of getting a dental impression somewhere on your body, or who are constantly fussing with their mouths—how are you supposed to deal with those biting habits?

Biting is a habit best stopped before it gets started. Some horse people have a very strict "no mouth" rule, in which the horse isn't allowed to touch humans with their mouths at all. This is the all-around safest option, but it does require a lot of strict enforcement.

"No mouth" contact means:

- No feeding your horse treats by hand

- No nose scratching

- No letting them play with your zippers, jackets, hats, or other pieces of clothing

- No face or body sniffing

Personally, I find it less stressful for both horses and humans to create a command that means "cease and desist." A horse is allowed to sniff me up close to get an idea of what's going on, but when I use the command, they know to stop. This can vary from horse to horse. Red responds when I say "gentle" or "quit." Belle listens when I make a game show buzzer noise.

That being said, neither Red nor Belle is a habitual biter. I have worked with many habitual biters over the years, and "no mouth" training can be helpful for horses who have an "all or nothing" attitude.

What causes habitual biting behavior? Generally, it's the usual suspect of boredom or improper diet. But just like kicking, humans can accidentally encourage the behavior by trying to make it stop. "I'll give you a treat if you stop biting" is not vocabulary a horse readily understands. Instead, you need to find a phrase that both you and your horse understand as "knock that off right this instance or so help me."

You may wish to call in a trainer or behaviorist to help you with a biter, if only for the fact that horses who like to bite can be sneaky about it, and it helps to have someone "watching your six" so to speak, so you don't get a posterior nip. Sometimes horses respond best if you act like another horse and "nip back," using a small riding bat; however, if you don't have the experience to get the timing and level of punishment equal to the crime, you and your horse may benefit from professional intervention.

There are also many humane muzzles available at equine specialty shops that simply clip onto a halter. Like grazing muzzles– which can also be employed in this manner– these muzzles allow horses to eat and drink and breathe normally. They simply prevent the teeth from making contact with anything besides food, water, air, and the inside of the muzzle.

Dealing with Bad Barn Behavior

You may be looking over the past several chapters thinking, "Ok, so if my horse starts doing any of these things, I should contact the vet and then see if my horse is bored?"

In a word: yes.

This seems very over-simplified, but think of a horse as having the communication skills of a toddler, powered by a millennium of survival instincts. If a toddler is trying to tell you why they're upset, they aren't going to say, "Oh, I beg your pardon. I know you're already occupied with your troubles, but may I have a moment of your time? I'd like to discuss with you some potential changes that might be beneficial to both of us." Instead, they cry, wail, and get violent in desperation.

Like toddlers, horses are also prone to reacting more strongly to a situation than it necessarily warrants. Horse tantrums are often the cause of explosive bad behavior, and result from not having the right information to make a rational decision. A horse doesn't know why it's bored; it simply knows that it would like to be anywhere other than its stupid stall doing nothing right now because that is simply unbearable on a cellular level. A horse also can't help itself rinse off boo-boos and ask for a Band-Aid, either. It simply knows that it's in pain, and this is a threat to its survival.

When a horse is behaving poorly in their stall, it's never a bad idea to run this information past your vet, especially if this is a brand new (or brand new to you) behavior. If Fluffy has never once shown you his teeth, and this morning he ripped a sleeve off your jacket, there's likely more than boredom at fault.

To that end, all of these habits are hard to stop, which makes prevention the best way to avoid them. If you notice your horse is acting a little grumpier or mopier than usual, mentally bookmark that behavior to see if it changes. Horses can absolutely have a bad day, just like we do, and snap back to whatever their version of "normal" is the next day. But if your horse has a bad day, then a worse day, after a month of this new grumpy attitude, starts nipping at everyone who walks down the aisleway, there is likely something they have been trying to bring to your attention for a while.

There is still quite a bit about equine mental health that we don't understand yet, but we're working on it. While we don't necessarily understand the causes or genetic probability of stable vices like cribbing or pawing, and we may not even be able to fully stop them, the equine community generally accepts that horses who have stable vices need something, don't like something, or have something to say about their current circumstances.

Unfortunately, horses sometimes have to make do with the terms of domestication. I have worked in many barns where free-roaming regular turnout simply wasn't a possibility, usually due to the area in which the barn was situated. You may not have dozens of horses and pastures to choose from to create the ideal situation for your horse. There may be weeks when you don't have meaningful interaction because you and your family got sick, then you had a huge presentation at work, and your car broke down... the list can go on and on.

Nearly every horse I've met has had to deal with some of the limitations of domestication at some point. As long as they're being fed, have plenty of clean water, and have a proper safe space in which to live, most of them get over temporary bouts of bad behavior. However, if your horse is frequently telling you that they are stressed out, you might want to consider what types of long-term changes you can make to compromise with them a bit.

It is also unrealistic to tell people to change their entire lives to accommodate a horse's stress level. It truly is a dance of compromise, and many horses can be taught to appreciate a different schedule or living situation than the ideal they've cooked up with their instincts.

That doesn't mean that you should ignore your horse's complaints because they're "just" bored. Compromise means action on both parties' behalf, so consider adding enrichment toys and tools to your horse's life, finding someone who enjoys giving your horse attention when you can't, and other small ways in which you can give your horse a little more stress relief.

Of course, just as a toddler rarely wants what they think they want, you may find yourself trying many different things to appease your horse. That is part of the journey, but once they find something they like, it usually takes them at least a few weeks to decide they don't like it after all!

Chapter Four

Handling Issues

Handling issues are very different from barn vices in many different ways. Typically, a horse with bad stall habits will leave those behaviors behind once they've left the stall. In most cases, they manifest when a horse is stressed out or can't think of anything better to do. Red, for example, will crib just about anywhere unless he has something else to keep his mind and mouth busy.

Handling issues also very rarely have anything to do with boredom, unless your horse has become so stressed out by their continued boredom that they act out at every potential opportunity. Instead, acting up when being led, tied, or when being asked to be polite around humans is nearly always a sign of pain, trauma, or poor training. As a result, it can be corrected with appropriate, safe, consistent, and patient training.

That sounds pretty straightforward on the surface, and in many cases it is. Once you have politely explained to your horse how you expect them to behave on a lead line, lunge line, or when tied, many of them appreciate that it is in their best interest to "be cool" and stand still and move only as asked. You may have to remind them several times, especially when the weather changes or your horse is excited about some recent development like the garbage collectors being outside or a dog running in the far, far distance, but many horses have been convinced that their feet don't have to move when their eyes and head do.

There are different ways to accomplish good handling behaviors, ranging from human body language to potentially dangerous methods. I personally prefer to start with the mildest option and escalate as necessary. This method is frequently referred to as "ask, tell, demand."

Let's break that down a little more:

1. Ask: In this stage, body language is neutral. I provide a clear scenario for the horse, such as clipping a lead rope to its halter and walking forward. It is not unreasonable for a human to say, "Hey, let's go over here" and expect the horse to follow.

2. Tell: If the horse doesn't respond immediately when I "ask" the first time, I will typically ask again. They may have been distracted or misinterpreted the question. If they still don't respond, that request becomes an instruction. "We are going over here." I will position my body so that the horse is very aware of the direction in which I'd like them to go. I might give the lead rope a brief, tight tug to make it abundantly clear that a response is required.

3. Demand: If the horse still refuses to respond appropriately, then it's time to switch gears from simply doing something with the horse to making this a learning opportunity. If the horse digs their feet in and refuses to move, tries backing up rapidly, and does everything in their physical power to avoid what I'm asking them, it is appropriate to escalate the situation. Once horses have clicked into instinct mode to avoid a command, it can be hard to bring them back to rational

mode. Sometimes it takes a quick physical cue, such as a pop on the shoulder with the end of the lead rope, or an assistant with a lunge whip coming up behind them to remind them that "yes" is a good answer.

There is no beating or punishment in the "ask, tell, demand" strategy. At first, it may seem that there's little difference between using a lunge whip to get a horse to move out of a dangerous situation and beating it silly. However, as you gain experience with equine behavior, you'll note that whips do not need to make contact with the horse to be effective. In most cases, horses will be motivated by the mere appearance of a whip or the motion from the lash.

That being said, there are times when you may find a little extra sternness is required to snap the horse out of whatever instinctual state they're in. Remember how horses communicate with each other in the wild—there can be a lot of well-placed, well-timed kicks and bites to help herd members understand what's happening and what their role is. A perfectly timed pop of a humane device like a crop or a quick shanking motion from a lead rope with a chain can simulate this type of communication to get your horse's attention back on you.

If a horse is completely lost in the sauce of relying on their instincts, a responsible horseperson has to help them find its way back to reality. Just like a toddler or a coworker having a bad day, it's important to keep a horse from injuring themselves or others when they're having a tantrum. Unfortunately, unlike a toddler or coworker, a hug or a piece of chocolate is not going to bring a horse back to reason.

Instead, many experts recommend getting a horse to move their feet to remind them there is still quite a bit to be done. Forward, backward, in circles—whatever keeps your horse from focusing on what they have deemed terrifying or unforgivable and prevents them from potentially injuring themselves on any nearby obstacles. Some-times a loud voice helps get their attention, too. Essentially, the goal is to provide the horse with something to think about besides its own discomfort at the original request. Keep their feet moving, and even-tually, the horse will wonder "Hey, why are we doing this?" Eventually, they'll stop resisting and look to the human for answers about what's happening and why. Thus the cycle starts over again until the horse agrees that the original request wasn't that silly after all.

This process takes a lot of trust—first, the horse needs to trust that the human isn't going to feed them to a monster or torture them. Second, human needs to trust their own instincts and ability to correct this behavior without accidentally escalating it into a more dangerous or severe situation.

If you do not trust that you are the individual to help guide your horse to trust and safety through these important steps in their train-ing, it's a great idea to contact a professional. Fear not—I've included a guide on finding and getting to know the right trainer for your horse in the next section.

For now, let's take a look at some of the common areas in which horses exhibit bad behavior, and what you can do to curb the naugh-tiness before it becomes an intense issue.

Standing Still and Being Tied

There are many reasons why we need our horses to stand still, whether or not they're tied to anything. Some common scenarios in which it would be preferable for a horse to stand still calmly and quietly include:

• Grooming

- Tacking up

- Assessing potential injuries

- Bathing

- Judging in the show pen

- Traveling in a trailer

- Waiting for a human who is going to the bathroom/talking to someone/dealing with another horse/any number of human activities that are much easier if our horses stand still for 1-3 minutes without causing mischief!

If you need to dismount and move an obstacle on a trail ride, it's great if your horse will stand still. If you fall off, it's absolutely wonderful if your horse doesn't run off. In fact, with a little time and patience, most horses can be convinced that standing still is the correct answer whenever they don't know what to do.

Not wanting to stand tied is frequently a training gap. In my decades of working with horses, I've found there are quite a few barns that simply do not have a place to tie a horse. In fact, one barn at which I worked strictly forbade tying a horse. At that facility, horses who exited their stalls either had to ground tie, which means standing still upon command and not moving until told otherwise,, or being held by another individual unless they were being ridden. There were 6-8 stable assistants on the clock at all times to accomplish this, too. As a result, it is entirely possible to find a horse who has made it to an advanced age without having been tied to a solid object.

Trauma is another reason why horses may not stand still. If they've had a bad experience when tied, it's understandable that they may not want to try that again, especially if that experience had nothing to do with their own behavior. Horses can slip when tied in a wash rack during bathing, or get tangled up when their tie comes loose or is improperly fashioned. Something scary may have happened to them when they were tied up and because they were stuck in one spot, they couldn't react the way they wanted to. Remember, horses want to get away from danger first, not stand still and check it out. Being tied definitely hampers this instinct, and some horses aren't sure what to do about it.

When a horse breaks free of any type of restraint, their instinct is to bolt around brainlessly. Some of them run merrily and purposefully savor their freedom for a few moments until they realize they would be completely lost without their herd. Red is in this group—on the few occasions he has escaped, the entire ordeal has lasted less than two minutes on average, and he'll either come up to me or the herd to admit that was fun, but he'd like to go back to his regular schedule now.

Other horses really do seem to lose their brains, galloping blindly at high speeds without much of a clue as to where they're going, and only calming down once everyone stops chasing them. This is Belle. She's not an escape artist, but if she finds herself unattended, she panics and runs. People following her yelling and shaking food are even more upsetting and drive her into a further panic.

And then there are the triumphant escapees. These horses look for a reason to roam, and they don't relinquish their freedom easily. I once had a Tennessee Walking Horse who would go on grand adventures by himself. Thankfully, the property had a main gate to keep him away from the road, but everyone needed to handle him with both eyes open so he wouldn't gallop off.

Standing still and being tied often occur in conjunction, but they're still two different skills for a horse to learn. Horses in the wild don't spend a lot of time standing still; after all, they graze and wander around 10-20 miles each day. They also don't encounter a lot of restrictions. If a feral horse can't move, then something is very wrong!

As a result, many horses aren't thrilled about learning these two skills. You may have to break the process down into many little steps with them as you work to assure them it really is ok to stand still, and being tied to something isn't the end of the world.

I once worked with a recently retired racehorse who was oddly head shy, meaning he didn't like things touching his face and head. I have no idea what happened to him in the past, but whenever he felt pressure on the backs of his ears, he went ballistic. He'd raise his head as high as possible, then bolt backward to break free of whatever was pressing on his head. He also pulled the crossties out of the wall. Usually anchored with heavy-duty screws, crossties are designed to hold a horse still in the aisleway of a barn. This particular pair was made of lightweight chains, so after he bolted, they jingled merrily behind him, further driving his terror. We went through many bridles and break-away halters, both of which are made of leather and snap easily in case of emergency.

It is more or less impossible to accommodate head shyness in a working horse. This horse had a decent career on the track, retired sound, and was now working beautifully under saddle dabbling in a little dressage and jumping to see what he enjoyed best. As a result, he needed to be able to hold himself together while his halter and bridle were interchanged at least twice a day.

While I worked with him on accepting the sensation of touch on his face, head, and neck, I also taught him to ground tie. With the command "tie," he knew that he was supposed to stand still until I clucked and snapped at him to come towards me. I also spent a lot of time working with him on the lead rope, encouraging him to follow me around. Eventually, the lead rope came off, and he habitually followed me around as I cleaned and watered the arena.

He learned these behaviors faster than he unlearned his head shyness. Still, it worked to my advantage when he snapped the crownpiece of his bridle during a lunging session. The minute he realized he didn't know what he was doing, he stopped and ground-tied himself until I came up to him and made a makeshift halter out of the lunge line. He did this again during a training session in the cross-ties. After he reared and snapped his halter, he stopped and stood still to be collected.

Eventually, he learned to agree that a little pressure on the back of his ears wasn't as dangerous as he had originally believed, and stood in the crossties like a model equine citizen. However, I'm very grateful that training him to stand still was so helpful—and comparatively simple.

If you have a horse who does not appreciate standing still and goes wild at the mere implication of being tied, you are not alone. The main goal when dealing with these behaviors is to convince the horse that these requests aren't unreasonable, torturous, or even mean-spirited. In fact, they're downright beneficial to the horse, though they fly in the face of every instinct the horse may have.

This means you might have to try different methods and approaches to the issue. When I say that the head-shy racehorse "eventually" learned, I mean "over the course of a year." Overcoming trauma is hard for all of us, so it's not realistic to expect a horse to say, "Oh, well this person says it's ok, so I reckon I'll just do whatever they say," the first time you try to explain it to them.

Instead, accept that this isn't impossible, but you may need additional assistance and practical resources to help you gain your horse's trust.

Grooming Politely

A horse standing quietly tied is integral to a polite grooming session. In fact, there might be a bit of a chicken/egg relationship between quiet tying and politeness during grooming, since it can be hard to tell which begets the other.

Ideally, you will be able to put your horse in cross ties or other secure ties, or even ground tie them and groom them. Grooming includes using a variety of specialized brushes and tools to maintain a horse's coat and skin health by removing mud, manure, and dead hair, as well as picking the hooves to remove mud and rocks. Grooming can help stimulate blood flow, redistribute skin oils, and create the right balance of elements to keep your horse looking glossy. This is also our opportunity to run our hands over our horses to check for lumps, bumps, scratches, or signs of skin problems, like crusty fungus plaques or patches of dry, flaking skin, hoof abscesses, or signs of thrush.

Horses also use grooming as an opportunity to act like fools. It is your job to evaluate whether this reaction is due to fear, excitement, boredom, or lack of training. Let's take a look at some of the common grooming tasks to dig deeper into the many ways and reasons why a horse can misbehave during a grooming session.

Brushing

If horses had an online forum, brushing would likely be one of the most divisive topics. Some horses absolutely adore being scrubbed down with a stiff, hard brush. Others would be pleased if they never had to endure it ever again.

There are many causes for this. Some horses– my own Red includ-ed– have thin, sensitive skin. They may shudder or bounce away from a particularly vigorous brushing, or threaten a nip or kick if you get too enthusiastic. In most cases, sensitive horses won't do more than issue a "hey, I don't like that" warning... unless you don't listen to them.

If your horse normally stands tied like a proper equine citizen but starts acting up when the brushes come out, they might be trying to tell you that you're doing it wrong. Of course, that doesn't mean you're doing it wrong according to any professional equine organi-zation, but by the horse's own level of preference. Try changing up your grooming routine, by using different brushes, or simply using the brushes differently, such as a lighter/shorter/longer/ stroke.

Remember also that warning nips and cocking the hoof in a manner that should remind you of a kick can be signs that the horse is in pain. If your horse continues to express sensitivity when brushing around the belly and tightening the girth, you might consider ulcers and consult with your vet for treatment suggestions. Likewise, a horse who is sore in its back or body might be saying, "No work today, please. Just rest."

Your horse may also dance in place while being groomed. Most of the time, this is the horse expressing impatience. Some horses do this because they really love their jobs, and they can't wait to get to work. Others do this because they are genuinely uncomfortable with the grooming process on a psychological level.

In either case, the best thing you can do to keep everyone safe is to not escalate the situation. Consider your horse a crate of dynamite in this instance. Do not light the match. Stay calm, be patient, get out of the way, and look for a way you can remove your horse from the situation so you can help them work out their feelings safely. My personal favorite is a lunge line session in a big arena, but work with what you've got– a round pen, a small paddock, or any other area where a horse can do all of the things their instincts are screaming at them to do, such as a bolt, run, and fight.

Some horses go through their life needing a little icebreaker session between the stall or pasture and hopping in the cross ties. I've known several horses who had to be lunged the moment they came out of their stalls for several minutes before their human could consider tying them up to be groomed or tacked up. This isn't necessarily naughty behavior, but more of a biological process. Think of the steps you take to go from bed to productivity, and you might be a little more sympathetic to your horse's needs.

Also, bear in mind that most horses will shift their weight a bit when being brushed. Many horses will move their bodies so that you are guaranteed to hit their itchy spots. Some will turn their heads so they can watch you, especially if they're in a new place. They might occupy their time by checking out whatever is going on around them, especially if there are windows, doors, or other horses nearby. Belle stands stock-still when being groomed, and it honestly creeped me out at first. I'm used to horses treating this as an interactive process!

Speaking of interactive grooming, your horse may try to groom you as a sign of their appreciation. It may be disheartening to discourage this practice since your horse truly thinks they're being nice, but human skin is not designed to take on even the gentlest of horse nibbles. In most cases, a light tap on the snoot with a gentle reprimand is enough to dissuade them, but I have met a few horses who are grumpy co-groomers and absolutely insist. Just like everyone else, your horse needs to learn to take "No" for an answer– just remember the "ask, tell, demand" method here to avoid escalating this conversation into a brawl.

Picking Hooves

"Picking hooves" is the act of using a tool—aptly named the hoof pick–to clean out a horse's hooves. Regardless of whether your horse wears shoes or not, the natural structure of the hoof can allow for rocks and all sorts of pasture debris to build up in the crevices. In the wild, horses spend most of their time moving, which causes this debris to crumble or work its way out. This is true for domesticated horses as well, but before you start working, your horse would really appreciate it if you could help them keep their feet clean.

Unfortunately, the anatomical mechanics of picking hooves isn't entirely pleasant for horses or humans. The horse is asked to stand with their weight redistributed among three legs, pick up each hoof in succession, and stand there quietly while you do your best to dig around in their feet with a dull metal pick. The human asks the horse to lift each hoof, bent over in a position in which the face and hoof are aligned.

The most common naughty hoof behavior for horses is refusing to pick up the hoof at all, followed closely by picking up politely enough, then shifting all of their weight so that the burden that would normally go on that leg is now transferred to the unsuspecting, mostly upside down human.

Honestly, I can't blame them. There is nothing in their Rolodex of Instinct that addresses having their feet touched—this is purely a domesticated creature situation. There's nothing natural about the way we pick up their feet, and very few living beings cherish the idea of holding one of their legs in the air for any period of time.

However, picking hooves and, as we'll later discuss, farrier work, are necessary for keeping our equine companions happy and healthy.

Hoof bruises, abscesses, and other injuries can form when a horse's hoof is exposed to rocks, mud, and other organic material.

I recommend each new horse owner go very slowly when picking hooves for the first time. Many professionals wear a helmet and thick leather gloves when working with an unfamiliar horse because it is possible that the horse either doesn't know what's happening or knows what's happening and hates it. Either method can elicit a kick or some other type of frantic, fight-or-flight-based behavior.

Refusing to pick up the hoof can be another situation altogether. Let's not forget about our familiar "pain response" reasoning for bad behavior. If a horse simply won't shift their weight off of a particular hoof to pick it up, it may have a good reason for their actions.

When I first got Red, he refused to pick up his right hind leg. He was extraordinarily polite with the rest of his hooves, but we engaged in a mild battle when it came to that particular hoof. After some time, I noticed that he wasn't moving that leg as freely as the rest. The vet did some x-rays and we discovered he had major arthritis in his right hock, which is the large joint at the back of a horse's hind leg. (Fear not—there are anatomical guides in the Resources section!) The reason he didn't want to pick up his hoof was because the sustained position of holding his hoof in the air was painful.

Arthritis is common in horses who work for a living and can develop in any joint. Unlike other leg and hoof injuries, there will rarely be warmth or swelling to indicate there's a problem. Furthermore, there's no way to train a horse to ignore the pain of an arthritis flare-up—at least, none that I've discovered yet.

Instead, the best thing to do is accommodate the horse's range of motion and flexibility as much as possible. You may find it's easier to ask them to tip their hoof up on the toe without leaving the ground. You may become exceptionally fast at picking hooves, too, so they don't have to suffer for very long. It's a good idea to work with your vet and farrier to help teach you some tricks to help your arthritic horse find a comfortable position for hoof cleaning and maintenance.

As a side note, this also goes for humans and their pain levels. Bending over in a squatting position with your head facing down with a horse trying to lie on your back can be very uncomfortable, especially if you're already dealing with arthritis or pain issues of your own. This is another situation where you might wish to work with your vet and farrier to find a way for you and your horse to collaborate on the hoof-picking situation.

The only tried-and-true method of convincing a horse to pick up its feet is consistent, patient work. Once your horse has accepted that you will be touching its hoof, the next step is encouraging them to pick it up and hold it patiently in front of your face. This can be a daunting task, so if you don't feel like you're making headway, it's a great idea to call in a professional. Bear in mind also that your horse may not have learned this particular skill in their youth, or someone may have tried to show them in a less-than-courteous way.

Bathing

The good news is that a majority of horses don't need to be bathed frequently. The bad news is that horses can find many things to object to when it comes to the bathing process.

Depending on your horse's job, the season, and any particular skin and coat needs your horse has, the bathing process may be pretty quick, or long and involved. For example, when Red was covered in rain rot, a type of equine skin fungus, we spent a lot of time doing specialized baths to help encourage the skin to heal quickly. For the purpose of our discussion, let's consider basic bathing to include:

1. Get horse wet

2. Add soap, lather

3. Rinse

4. Repeat as needed

You may wish to wash the body, mane, and tail at the same time, or separately, as necessary for what you're trying to accomplish.

The easiest way to bathe a horse is with a hose; however, the serpentine nature of a common hose is often the first obstacle to overcome in this process. Many horses are terrified of hoses, especially when they hiss and spit without provocation. With time and patience, most horses will accept that hoses exist and are not lethal.

Then comes the "getting wet" part. While I have encountered a few horses who hate being wet, many have experienced rain, mud, snow, sweat, and other situations in which they've become damp. The part they don't like is the directed blast of water coming directly at them.

Horses tend to have a favorite hose setting, so take your time experimenting with the version your horse likes the best. When you turn on the hose, point it down so it won't spurt and jet directly onto your horse. You may choose to tie your horse or have another person hold onto their lead rope so your horse doesn't wander off. Red prefers to munch on grass and take a few long drinks from the hose during bath time, but we've already established that he's an odd one, so don't expect this right away.

The soap or shampoo part is rarely traumatic, but you will need to rinse it all away, so try to apply it evenly and not get too enthusiastic, especially if your horse is already impatient or uncomfortable with the process.

In fact, for many horses, the wash rack is the hardest mental obstacle to overcome. Wash racks traditionally involve a paved, angled floor with a drain. There may be rubber mats installed to help horses maintain traction because the combination of wet pavement and wet hooves often leads to a low-friction situation. A horse who can't get its feet under them and is simultaneously tied by the head can panic, and panic often leads to mayhem. Many horses have experienced some kind of wash rack accident, which leaves them prone to taking out their past trauma on future humans.

Depending on your barn rules, the wash rack might be optional. As I mentioned, Red likes outdoor baths. He loves the hose, and while he doesn't mind being tied in a wash rack, he'll stand politely without being tied as long as he has some grass to enjoy. That being said, you and your barn owner may not want to contend with the soapy, muddy patch of ground that comes with outdoor baths.

With time, kindness, and patience, most horses can grow to at least begrudgingly accept the occasional bath. This can be very helpful for us humans because cold-hosing is a common treatment for musculoskeletal issues like tendon injuries and flesh wounds, and it's much easier to hose down a horse who is accustomed to the process, rather than training as you go.

Grooming is, at best, a fun bonding activity between horse and human. It can also be a source of trauma and actual physical pain for horses. When working with a new horse, assume innocence and approach with caution. In many cases, you'll find that a horse catches on to these activities quickly and learns to enjoy them. However, if your horse starts acting up during the grooming process, it might be time to investigate why they're acting like this, and what you can do to help them feel more comfortable being tied up and fussed with for periods of time. After all, it's in their best interest!

Flying a Horse-Shaped Kite

When a horse acts up when being led, horse people occasionally joke about "flying a horse-shaped kite." Horses can prance, bolt, rear, try to spin around, kick, bite, and do all sorts of naughty things on the lead line that might make you feel like you're trying to catch a kite in a hurricane. The goal is to teach them that none of this is appropriate.

The dangers of a horse who acts up while being led are plentiful and obvious. If the horse manages to get loose, chaos can reign until they are collected and corralled in a safe area. They can easily injure themselves or anything in their path as they fuss and stomp and kick their way from Point A to Point B.

If you've ever watched a high-performance equine competition, such as barrel racing, or show jumping, or even been to the racetrack, you've probably seen eager horses acting like this as they make their way to the pen. These horses aren't necessarily misbehaving—they're stoked and ready to go. Like boxers warming up next to the ring before a fight, or football players passing balls back and forth to stay limbered up during their time on the field, these horses are pep-talking themselves and keeping their muscles warm. They're in the zone, and you can tell because they are typically eager to go where you're pointing them.

Horses who have less demanding jobs can also display these behaviors when going somewhere fun, like the pasture or the trails. In many cases, this is unintended impoliteness. Still, it's important to teach a horse that such behavior is not necessary.

Logically speaking, a horse who can be taught to stand still can be taught to walk calmly from one place to another. Many times a firm hand and a few well-timed "NO" commands will get the point across. But every once in a while, a horse will forget their manners on the lead line. As a human who regularly interacts with the horse, it's important to take the next possible opportunity to have a deep discussion about what ground manners are all about. It is always easier to accommodate a horse's preferences than reinforce manners. In some cases, like hoof-picking on a horse in pain, that's necessary. But there's really no good reason you should have to regularly fly a horse-shaped kite.

On the other hand, many horses think throwing a complete tantrum will get them what they want. Like a child pitching a fit over a piece of candy in the grocery store checkout lane, they will do whatever they can to not have to go where you want them to or to do what you want them to do. And while children are relatively moveable in these instances, horses weigh a lot more.

Therefore, setting and continue practicing your horse's ground manners are extremely important for horses and humans alike. I've included a few links in the Resources section to get you started with some groundwork basics, but the principles are as follows:

- A horse should walk on a lead rope politely and quietly, matching your pace

- Horse should keep their teeth and hooves to themselves while being led

- A horse should stand still when you stand still

- A horse should back up when cued

- A horse should move towards or away from you as cued

The primary tools in leading a horse are a halter and a lead rope. The halter is made of several straps that go around the top of the head, nose, and jaw. A lead rope is a heavier, longer rope that clips to one of the various rings on the halter, depending on what you're doing. Some lead ropes include a length of chain, known as "stud chains." I do not recommend inexperienced folks use a lead rope with a chain until they know what to do with it and how to properly fasten it. There are many ways you can purposefully use a chain to reinforce good behavior and even more ways that it can cause damage if things get out of control.

Groundwork is honestly my favorite part of working with untrained horses. It's equal parts art, science, and observation. Each horse is unique in their approach to learning. Some horses pick it up right away while others insist on fighting the system. In many cases, these fights are communication issues, and by really paying attention to what a horse is saying, we can more clearly and calmly discuss the issue at hand.

A horse who follows behind you calmly is highly beneficial not simply because it's less of a pain in the neck, but because there can be situations in which you need a horse to follow you, no questions asked. This is the framework that will allow you to lead a horse through questionable terrain on the trail, into a trailer, and away from scary things that may or may not be dangerous. Groundwork is the basis for all your communication with your horse, so teaching a horse good manners and continuously reinforcing that behavior is essential to becoming a good equine citizen.

The amount of patience that is needed to persuade a large, instinct-laden creature to trust you is immense, but the reward of earning that trust is exceedingly fulfilling. Plus, mitigating the danger and frustration that comes with trying to control an antsy, dancing beast is a great bonus.

The Model Equine Citizen

Handling issues are quite common, and often come and go depending on your horse's mood and what's going on at that moment. Horses can get excited if something new and interesting is happening, like a new horse on the property, the farrier or vet coming to visit, or the chaos of preparation for a show. In my personal opinion, it's acceptable for a horse to have feelings about something that's going on and demonstrate a momentary lapse in politeness. The horse is not, however, permitted to go brainless and potentially create a dangerous situation.

At the core of every model equine citizen is a horse who has a solid background in groundwork. That's not to say that these horses don't experience occasional fits of whimsy, but that they regularly behave in a safe, appropriate manner, and know when to knock it off. Ultimately, you can tell whether a horse is being naughty, or just having a moment by how they respond to correction.

All horses should know the word "no," or a command of your choice that has the same meaning. "Stop." "Quit." "HEY BOZO KNOCK IT OFF!" Whatever you and your horse agree is the most appropriate way to get their attention verbally is great, though I advise against teaching a horse colorful language if you're going to be taking them to public events or riding locations. On the other hand, you'll just be saying what we're all thinking, so I'll let you decide on the commands you teach your horse at your own discretion.

If you ask your horse to quit acting as if they have never been taught manners and they do not quit, then tell them. If necessary, demand that they stop. At the same time, you don't want to cause the situation to escalate. A good equine citizen will know when they should stop, which is why groundwork training is absolutely imperative in my eyes and those of many equine professionals.

Ground manners come into play all the time. Any time someone enters your horse's stall, whether to handle them, clean, or feed them, you want your horse to be polite. No nipping, kicking, or threatening behavior. Any time someone leads your horse, you want them to follow along graciously, paying attention to directions like "stop," "walk," and "turn around." You want them to tie patiently and relax for the grooming process. You want to be able to fuss with your horse and touch every inch of its body without resistance.

Consider also your farrier and your veterinarian. They would also prefer to interact with your horse without fear of mortal peril. A horse who will stand still patiently can be inspected and treated by either professional more quickly and accurately than one who won't settle down. While most vets can provide a tranquilizer to help keep a horse calm during farrier work, this can get costly, and it may be difficult to coordinate schedules with your farrier and vet every time your horse needs their feet touched.

Then there's anyone who might potentially come in contact with your horse. If you board at a larger facility, that can potentially mean anyone in the barn at the most, and the team of barn employees at the minimum. If you have a working horse, like Belle and Red, they need to understand how to be courteous to everyone they come in contact with, regardless of age, size, and experience, to minimize risk in a lesson facility.

Even if your horse lives in your backyard, and you're the only person who ever touches them, it's a great idea to teach and reinforce good manners. If anything should happen to you, your facility, or your horses, you don't want anyone to have a problem keeping your horses out of harm's way. Consider natural events, like hurricanes and tornadoes, which can blow apart barns and relocate fencing. Disasters like fires and floods can also create an emergency where your horse has to listen to someone else.

I strongly believe—and there are many like me—that good ground manners are essential for every horse. Furthermore, I think every horse has the capability of learning them, though, like humans, some horses need more frequent and direct reinforcement than others.

I also strongly believe that humans can take training too far. Facing off against thousands of years of finely developed instinct is not an easy task, and it takes a lot of trial and error. Explaining things to a 1,000-pound animal requires time, patience, tenacity, bravery, quietness, sternness, determination, grace, sympathy, openness, understanding, discipline, and steel resolve. As a result, I would say that certain people are more equipped to train than others.

As I've noted multiple times, contacting a professional is a great idea...as long as you connect with the right professional. Let's take a look at the process so that you can find the right person to help you and your horse learn together.

Quick Guide: How to Choose a Professional to Help You

In my decades of experience with horses, I have found that it is very easy to know when you're outmatched and need a little help working with your horse. It can be difficult to find a vet, farrier, trainer, behaviorist, cowboy, or other equine expert to assist you.

That's not to say that there aren't plenty of people who are willing to share their advice. If you say "My horse has started doing XYZ" in a room populated with other horse people, you will likely get dozens of unsolicited recommendations, tips, and tricks on how to help resolve the situation. Horse people tend to have lots of opinions about how things should be done because they have all discovered methods that work for them. We are a very eager type, and we would like to help you solve your problems.

As a result, it can be either too easy or too hard to trust someone who claims to be an expert horse trainer. I hesitate to use the word "expert" when referring to myself because even though I've worked with hundreds of horses in many different capacities over the past 30-plus years, I still have a lot to learn. I have a toolbox full of activities and resources I can apply when working with an unfamiliar horse, but I also recognize that there are going to be some problems I simply cannot solve.

At the same time, I'm also very picky about who can work with my horses in a training capacity. I know my horses and their triggers, and I know what types of things will escalate a situation rather than resolve it. I also know when Belle and Red are actually being naughty, and when their behavior is likely trying to tell me something is amiss.

Therefore, the first step I would recommend to any new horse owner is to learn about your animal. Figure out if their behavior is based on sheer orneriness, pain, boredom, bad training, trauma, or a combination of a few. You might be shocked to discover how much a horse can remember.

Horses have personalities, too. Learning your horse's general character can help you gain insight into which behaviors need attention and which are just another side of their natural charm.

Knowing your horse means you can address issues as they arise. If your horse is trying to tell you about a stressful issue in their life, you'll recognize their new behavior as a symptom, rather than a training issue. That, in turn, can help you reach out to the correct professional to assess the situation.

But how do you know you've reached the right professional? There aren't a lot of licensing requirements or professional credentials among horse people. Veterinarians, of course, must complete schooling to earn their licenses, but what about anyone else who touches your horse? Farrier certifications are available, but not legally required for those working in the United States or Canada. That means that anyone with a rasp and a set of nippers can technically hang out their shingle as a professional farrier.

The same is true of trainers. It is possible to earn a degree in equine science or equine studies. A myriad of trainer and instructor certifications are available. But since these aren't required, quite literally anyone can say they're a professional horse person.

There are a few consequences to this, too. Equine insurance laws and regulations can vary from state to state, but usually, a facility that is open to the public is required to carry a certain amount of liability insurance for those other humans. The horse itself generally isn't covered by these types of policies, which means that allowing other people to work with your horse on your own property can be dangerous from a liability perspective. If anyone gets hurt or anything gets damaged, you might get caught up in a whirlwind of litigation.

Therefore, my second recommendation is to really research who you are inviting to help care for your horse. Learn about their reputation. Ask for their credentials. How long have they been doing this? Can they talk about their previous clients without gossiping? Do they have references who can attest to their work? Since we live in the Internet Age, this is actually easier than ever. A little Google, some Facebook and YouTube searches, and a few texts should help you get a good feeling about whether or not you should trust this alleged "professional."

Furthermore, a lot of people in the horse world know a lot of other people in the horse world. Some of the best recommendations I've received for my horses have come from the fellow who owns the local feed mill. The equine dentist he recommended is incredibly gentle, and Red thinks his chiropractor needs to snuggle every time she comes to see him. Bulletin boards are still in fashion at feed stores, tack shops, and other places where horse people tend to go. Ask if anyone has heard of a particular person. I know I just mentioned the Internet Age, but word-of-mouth networking is still very much alive and well in the equestrian community.

If you've heard decent things about a particular farrier, dentist, trainer, behaviorist, or other professional, the next thing to do is to reach out to them to get more insight into their philosophy and style of training.

Ask them questions like:

- **Who are your mentors? Where did you learn your skills?** This is especially important in trainers, as you'll have the ability to do further research on what we call "Big Name Trainers," or BNTs. A BNT is the type of trainer who does clinics across the country, appears in different publications, and typically has a glowing record of their accomplishments. Many local trainers emulate the methods of a BNT, and many BNTs have their own web pages or YouTube channels where they share their philosophies and practices. Learning how a BNT operates can help you decide whether this is a good fit for you and your horse, as well as how well the local version lives up to the legend.

- **What types of equipment do you use?** I personally do not like using rope halters, because they offer no release. I don't trust my own timing to prevent a panicking horse from fighting against a rope halter, which can cause injuries in the neck, back, and skull. Other professionals are absolutely brilliant with a rope halter, and I will happily allow them to handle my horses in one.

- **How do you evaluate a horse's needs?** You want someone who is going to pay attention to how your horse acts, reacts, communicates, observes, and learns. Even a farrier can learn quite a lot about a horse by watching them move a bit and feeling along their backs and legs to discover "hot spots." Equine body language is amazingly honest, so finding a professional who pays attention to subtle movements and expressions is instrumental to finding someone genuinely interested in working with your horse, rather than just adding another source of income to their books.

Other questions are equally important but may warrant less of a discussion than direct answers. These questions can include:

- How do you measure success?

- How much do you charge?

- How often do you recommend I use your services?

- How do I schedule appointments with you?

- Do you travel, or do I need to bring my horse to you?

- Will you give me homework/exercises I can do with my horse to increase their well-being?

Finally, but most importantly, get your horse's opinion. I know it sounds a little out there, but your horse will tell you if they don't like the professional you've chosen. Red has traditionally loved his vets. He knows that they are the harbingers of feeling good, and he is truly on his best behavior when he knows that a vet is on the premises. One of his earliest vets referred to him as her "boyfriend" because he always greeted her with a nicker and a cuddle. So imagine my surprise when he danced around the aisle impatiently when I introduced him to the vet who originally serviced my current barn. As I tried to explain his medical history, Red shifted and shimmied up and down the aisleway, starting conversations with horses through stall doors and shoving me around. I'd had Red for ten years at that point, so I knew it wasn't his typical response to anything, much less a vet.

However, this particular vet was very high-energy. He spoke loudly and rapidly, rarely letting anyone else speak. He was constantly fidgeting, so Red started fidgeting along with him. I think everyone involved was grateful when that vet retired and was replaced by a mild-mannered vet who is tall enough to give Red scratchy scratches at the top of his head while occasionally doling out peppermints for very good horses.

If you have chosen a professional for your horse, be it a vet, farrier, dentist, trainer, behaviorist, communicator, or rider, make sure your horse is on board with this decision. Much as a toddler might act out when faced with an authority figure that scares them, horses will react to people they don't like. This is completely counterintuitive to what the professional is supposed to be doing, so if your horse is aggravated by your selection, it might be time to find a new professional.

It may seem that every person who has successfully convinced a horse to change their mind about a particular task tends to think that they're a fantastic trainer. To their credit, anyone who can help a horse understand something other than their innate method of conduct is something of a miracle worker, and that accomplishment should not be diminished.

However, actually working with a horse in a meaningful, corrective, and acceptable way truly requires a significant amount of experience, as well as an open mind, plenty of energy, and thick boots. You may need to interview several prospective professionals before you find just the right fit for you and your horse.

Once you have chosen just the right person, make sure you're both aware of the agreement. Before you sign anything, you'll both want to decide:

- What services they will provide

- How you will each measure the success of their service

- The price per service and any additional fees

- What insurance coverage do you each have, and how it co-ordinates in the event of an unexpected situation

- The timeframe in which you can expect results

You will likely experience many surprises as you and your horse continue to work with professionals throughout your journey together. The best way to prepare for these surprises is to be transparent and communicative with each party. Make sure you're involved in your horse's progress, and pay attention to any clues your horse may be giving you about issues along the way.

Conclusion

At this point, you might be feeling an overwhelming sense of gratitude that your horse doesn't display all of these behaviors. Feel free to set this book down for a moment so you can hug your equine companion and let them know how you feel.

On the other hand, you might lump in your stomach, having learned that your horse's behavior is something you need to address now, rather than hoping it just stops. I completely sympathize. Horses have the uncanny ability to make us drain our pocketbooks and stay up all night worrying, and yet we love them for it.

It is possible to help a horse find new and healthy ways to express their emotions and connect with their instincts. Horses can be trained – we've been doing it for thousands of years. Just because you're over-faced and anxious at this moment does not mean all hope is truly lost.

I know I've said this several times, but it's important to reiterate: horses are living beings. They have good days and bad days, and sometimes they act out just to test boundaries or let you know how they're feeling. It's when these actions become habits that problems arise, which is why we need to address them at the onset.

Some habits cannot be trained away, like cribbing or weaving. However, you can work with your horse to alleviate whatever stress is causing them to indulge in these behaviors. At the very least, you can understand why they're doing what they're doing and take a compassionate approach to their actions, instead of wondering why your horse is defective.

I honestly feel there is no such thing as a "defective" horse. Yes, they're weird. They do strange things. They can be goofy, grumpy, anxious, flirtatious, and mopey. But, if you take the time to really observe your horse in a variety of scenarios, you may find that they're not much different than we are—processing the world around them the best they can and trying to have a good time while they do it.

While there is certainly a limit to what each of us can do to make our horses happy, it is in our best interest to be kind stewards to our critters. That can mean investing extra time, energy, and money into working through their issues with a professional or finding a new situation for them that better suits their needs. A misbehaving horse is inconvenient, sure, but it's rarely a solid line drawn in the sand. Learn about your horse, develop communication with your horse, and eventually, the two of you will agree on how things are going to work out.

And when you do reach this agreement, there won't be enough hugs, treats, or scratchy scratches in the world to demonstrate how amazing it feels.

Resources

I know that this book went a bit quickly through some common horse knowledge that isn't so common outside of the horse world. Therefore, I've provided a series of resources that can help you do a deep dive into some of the topics I've mentioned.

While I've historically provided resources based on topics, some readers have asked that I try resources per section, so they don't have to jump around as much to find what they'd like to learn more about. I'm happy to give that option a try!

Please note that I am not associated with any of these websites, nor am I getting any commission for using these resources in this book. I do not guarantee anything that is mentioned in these resources, either. I have chosen these sites simply because I liked the way they explain the often-complicated world of equine instinct and behavior from an educational perspective, as well as their use of additional illustrations, videos, and links for those who really want to go down a research rabbit hole.

Resources for Section 1: Evolution, Instinct, and How Horses Behave in the Wild

These resources focus on the origin and development of horses to complement our discussion about equine ancestors in Section 1.

Domestication of the Horse :

https://en.wikipedia.org/wiki/Domestication_of_the_horse

Yes, it's a Wikipedia article, but the sources cited provide an additional scientific and informative insight into when, where, and how horses became part of our lives.

https://www.smithsonianmag.com/science-nature/when-did-humans-domesticate-the-horse-180980097/

This a compelling article regarding the evidence we have of equine domestication.

Anatomy and Physiology :

https://www.thesprucepets.com/the-parts-of-a-horse-1887388#:~:text=The%20muzzle%20is%20the%20part,is%20very%20mobile%20and%20sensitive

A pictorial guide to the parts of the horse can help you follow along with the various body parts I've mentioned.

https://www.equinespot.com/horse-anatomy.html

Here are several internal, external, structural, and hoof anatomy charts to help you become acquainted with your horse's body.

The United States Bureau of Land Management :

https://wildhorsesonline.blm.gov/

This resource is excellent for understanding the modern American Mustang, where they roam, and various conservation activities across the country.

Resources for Section 2: Causes of Naughtiness

In this section, we examined a few different reasons why a horse might be acting inappropriately, including pain, boredom, poor training, and trauma.

Equine Dentistry:

This comprehensive site explains the basics, right from the horse's mouth.

Equine Chiropractic :

https://ceh.vetmed.ucdavis.edu/news/chiropractic-care-horses
This article explains why and how horses see the chiropractor.

The Farrier :

https://www.thefarrierguide.com/p/what-does-farrier-do.html
This site offers a lot of information about hooves and horseshoeing, starting with the basics of what a farrier actually does for your horse.

Proper Tack and Equipment :

https://www.smartpakequine.com/content/saddle-fitting-guide
This article has some great photos and videos explaining how different types of saddles should fit your horse.

The following two articles include information about bits and bitting. I've included two links, as the first predominantly focuses on English riding styles, while the second is for Western riders.

https://horseyhooves.com/types-of-horse-bits/ (English and Western)

https://nrsworld.com/blogs/learning-center/types-of-bits (Western)

Equine Body Language :

https://equusmagazine.com/behavior/horse-body-language/
I like this article because it looks at each body part, as well as whole-body communication.

https://opensanctuary.org/understanding-horse-body-language-ears/?print=print
This article focuses on what a horse's ear position and movement can tell us about what's on their mind.

https://equimed.com/health-centers/behavior/articles/equine-language-facial-vocal-and-body#:~:text=The%20horse%27s%20muzzle%2C%20lips%2C%20nostrils,Wrinkled%20muzzle%3A%20nervous%2C%20worried

This article includes a bulleted list of different behaviors and what they might mean for quick reference.

Equine Abuse and Trauma Resources :

https://aaep.org/sites/default/files/Guidelines/AAEPFAQsEquin eAbuse.pdf

This is an actual veterinarian resource for identifying abuse in clients' horses, but it can also be helpful for those who suspect their horse may have been in a less-than-ideal situation in the past.

https://horserookie.com/tips-rehab-abused-horse/

Should you find yourself with a horse who has been rescued, you can find some practical tips for getting to know your new beast in this article.

Body Condition Scoring :

https://www.smartpakequine.com/learn-health/video/henneke-b ody-condition-scoring-video

This video walks through how to assess your horse's body condition score, and when to take action.

https://www.horsejournals.com/horse-care/feed-nutrition/henne ke-equine-body-condition-scale

Here you'll find diagrams that explain the body condition scoring process, as well.

Horse Guts and Gut Problems :

https://www.smartpakequine.com/learn-health/horse-digestion#: ~:text=Approximately%2070%20feet%20in%20length,first%20layov er%20is%20the%20cecum

This article includes a detailed artistic diagram as well as a basic review of the equine digestive processes, which can give you an idea of how things should work. (No photos)

https://ohioline.osu.edu/factsheet/1022 NOTE: ACTUAL BIO-LOGICAL PHOTOS

Here you'll find actual medical photos and descriptions of the equine digestive system along with common issues.

https://ceh.vetmed.ucdavis.edu/health-topics/equine-gastric-ulcer-syndrome NOTE: ACTUAL BIOLOGICAL PHOTOS

In this article, you'll learn more about gastric ulcers, along with photos from a gastric scope.

https://aaep.org/horsehealth/equine-gastric-ulcers-special-care-and-nutrition

This article explains gastric ulcers with no photos, in case you would rather not see that!

Resources for Section 3: Bad Barn Habits and How to Deal with Them

This section reviewed some of the ways horses can demonstrate bad behavior in the barn, as well as what they might be trying to communicate with their "nasty" habits.

Cribbing :

https://ceh.vetmed.ucdavis.edu/health-topics/cribbing

This insightful article is a great place to start for those dealing with a cribber for the first time.

Chewing :

https://equimed.com/health-centers/behavior/articles/is-your-horse-eating-your-barn

The photos that accompany this article demonstrate how drastic this habit can truly be.

Weaving :

https://www.helpfulhorsehints.com/horse-weaving/

This helpful article includes a video so you can see what weaving looks like.

Stall Walking :

https://equimed.com/diseases-and-conditions/reference/stall-walking

In addition to explaining the behavior in greater detail, this article includes links to more information about equine psychology.

Kicking and Pawing :

https://proequinegrooms.com/tips/grooming/the-inside-scoop-on-stall-kicking/

I like this article because it approaches the issue from the perspective of a professional groom. These are the individuals who handle horses in large facilities, which gives them a unique take on the issue.

https://www.horsefactbook.com/horse-care/horse-pawing-ground/

This article provides a little background on pawing, and why it can be a problem.

https://www.horsefactbook.com/trivia/how-hard-do-horses-kick/

I found this interesting, as it measures the force of a horse's kick versus other types of activities.

Biting :

https://ihearthorses.com/what-to-do-if-your-horse-bites-you-and-how-to-stop-it/

This article provides lots of great insight into biting and stopping this behavior without coming to fisticuffs.

More about Muzzles :

https://horseracingsense.com/best-grazing-muzzles/

A grazing muzzle's primary function is to reduce- but not prohibit- grass intake to prevent obesity and sugar processing issues in horses, but as we discussed in this chapter, there are many uses for a humane device like this. This page explains some of the different types and how they work.

Resources for Section 4: Handling Issues

This section deals with instilling good manners in your horse, so I've included a lot more resources for each topic covered in this section to help give you some more insight and background into basic groundwork.

Tying :

https://practicalhorsemanmag.com/health-archive/heres-30302/

A few thoughtful options for helping your horse understand the process of tying.

https://www.horseillustrated.com/horse-training-train-your-horse-to-tie

I appreciate how this article explains the steps of training a horse, as it really emphasizes how much patience can be required!

Grooming :

https://www.aqha.com/-/horse-grooming-basics

This is essentially a checklist for a basic– but thorough– grooming routine.

https://cowboymagic.com/40-horse-grooming-tips/

A comprehensive list that includes bathing and shows grooming tips in addition to grooming pointers.

https://horseandcountry.tv/horse-grooming-101-a-guide-for-beginners/#curry-comb

This article goes into significant detail about what each brush or tool is for, how to use it, and when to use it. There's a video master class at the end, as well.

https://www.sstack.com/blog/product-guides/the-ultimate-guide-to-horse-brushes/b/R0116/

A pictorial guide of various types of brushes, which you can also buy on this site (again, not affiliated).

Hoof Picking :

https://www.youtube.com/watch?v=2z2bb1syxjU&t=28s

If you are not familiar with the hoof-picking process, I strongly recommend watching this video to appreciate how intimidating it can be. There are some great tips in this video for enforcing good manners, too.

https://www.horseillustrated.com/horse-training-patient-hoof-picking

Another article presents helpful tips when picking hooves.

Groundwork :

I had to refrain from adding too many resources for groundwork because there are many great videos, articles, and trainer sites out there. I narrowed it down to these two because they take a very open, patient, yet firm approach to the groundwork. Furthermore, both sites are reputable resources for horse owners on all sorts of topics!

https://www.horseillustrated.com/herd-leader-through-groundwork

https://thehorse.com/136950/groundwork-with-our-horses-why-we-do-it/

Stud Chain :

https://learninghorses.com/horse-stud-chain/

This is just a quick article explaining how a stud chain works. Again, I would recommend not using one until you feel comfortable with the purpose and potential reaction.

The
Well-Mannered
Horse

Developing an Ideal Equine Buddy

Meredith Hill

Contents

Introduction

Ah, horses. Many of us are captivated by the beauty and grace of these majestic creatures. Horses are blessed with a natural elegance, and watching one gallop around evokes feelings of freedom, strength, and majesty Yet, underneath the glossy coats, velvety muzzles, and large expressive eyes are a myriad of opinions and instincts—not all of which align readily with the opinions and instincts of their human counterparts.

Furthermore, horses are large, wild animals. They're tall, muscular, and well-equipped with hooves that can kick and teeth that can bite. As big, fast-prey animals, they know a lot of ways to get away from objects and situations that they don't like or trust. And, while many of us on the human side of the discussion consider ourselves strong or fast, we are not horse strong or horse fast.

You've probably heard of the term "horsepower" when referring to vehicles, but have you ever wondered what "horsepower" really means? The term was coined by James Watt–the same guy after whom the measure of power is named. In the 1700s, Watt was attempting to compare the power of his newly re-engineered steam engine to the capability of the horses that might be replaced by the engine. He observed horses working to turn a mill wheel and determined that they turned the wheel 2.5 times per minute. Using the definition of "work" as energy transferred over a while, he calculated that one horsepower equals 33,000 foot-pounds of work per minute. You can think of this also as the power needed to lift an object that weighs 33,000 pounds one foot above the ground in one minute.

Modern calculations indicate that today's horses have an average of 15 horsepower. Humans, on the other hand, aren't quite as powerful. It's estimated that a very athletic human is capable of approximately 1.2 horsepower.

Physics and math are fascinating and all, but you're probably wondering what this has to do with horses and manners. My point is simple: you cannot win a tug-of-war match with a horse. It's simply not possible, given the rules of physics. You cannot run faster than they do or jump higher than they can, and with all of their hard-wired, finely-tuned instincts, it's not likely that you'll outwit them when they go into survival mode.

I recently wrote about how horses' instincts influence their behavior in my book *Why Does My Horse Act Like This: Understanding Equine Behavior in Your New Horse.* In that book, we examine how horses are biologically prepared to survive and how their instincts can dictate their behavior. Some of the bad habits our horse's display today are directly related to how they have evolved to stay alive in the wild.

So we've got this 15-horsepower critter with centuries of instincts, weighing in at approximately 1,000 pounds, and who is capable of speeds up to 40-50 miles per hour in one corner. In the other corner, a human. Two legs, flexible hands, 20 miles per hour on a good day. The goal is to create a partnership between the two, in which each party understands what the other is asking. What can we do to ensure the best possible rate of survival for the small, slow human?

This is where the well-mannered horse comes into the story. A horse that understands how its behavior impacts everything around it is still dangerous and unpredictable. However, a horse who understands its surroundings and other living beings, and has been taught how to behave safely, is less likely to create a dangerous situation.

They say that everyone has some sort of very strong, soul-crushing fear. Whether it can be categorically considered a phobia or not, nearly everyone has something about which they are irrationally fearful. For some, it's a fear of something that could be dangerous, like heights or swimming in the ocean. For others, it's something we can't explain, such as a fear of clowns or the number thirteen. I don't want to trigger anyone, so we won't go any further than that.

Instead, I want you to think of the way your strongest aversion makes you feel, and apply that to your horse. While we don't scientifically know exactly how horses feel when their prey instincts kick in, I like to assume that it's a deep, illogical aversion or fear that starts somewhere in their very DNA. I can identify with that feeling, and it helps me appreciate what might be running through a horse's mind and body when it's faced with something new and potentially dangerous.

What we hope to accomplish, by teaching a horse good manners, is instilling that same inner voice that tells us that while our fear might be real, the situation is not nearly as dangerous as we think it is. If we can convince ourselves not to have a meltdown when we encounter something terrifying, surely we can help our horses understand that being afraid isn't always a call to action. We've learned how to observe, analyze, and act accordingly. Teaching our horses the same is safer for us and better for them in the long run.

But there are a few cracks in this plan. First of all, horses don't exactly speak human languages. They communicate through body language, breath, nickers, whinnies, and snorts. Then there's that size difference thing again. How are we supposed to sit down and explain plastic bags to our horses in an empathetic yet assertive manner?

Instilling good manners in your horse is not an easy task, but it is incredibly important, for your safety and the safety of anyone—or anything—that may come in contact with your horse. You need to be able to harness the 15 horsepower that lives on four legs to keep risk to a minimum.

In this book, we'll continue to build on knowledge of equine needs, behaviors, and instincts with an introduction to good manners, and what is considered a "well-mannered horse." We'll look at what we can reasonably expect from our horses and some of the ways we can help our horses understand what we're asking.

I don't claim to have all the answers, and reading this book will not elevate you to Big Name Trainer status overnight. What I hope to do is provide you with a few suggestions so you can evaluate and address your horse's manners in a way that is safe and practical for you and your horse.

That might mean involving a trainer or equine professional who can help you establish and maintain good behavior. To that end, I've included a discussion regarding the huge grey area surrounding appropriate training methods, and the equally concerning boundaries between reinforcement and abuse. I've learned from my readers' emails that you are very concerned about equine well-being, and worried about certain training methods. That's why we'll take a look at some of the realities of horse training to prepare you for selecting a professional to assist you, should you choose to go that route.

I wish I had the magical power to make a wish and grant everyone who reads this a well-mannered horse. In fact, I wish I had the magical power to make my own fuzzy beasts behave 100% of the time. Instead,

I have worked with them for years and will continue to work with them to help them make the best decisions they can when strange things happen. Still, they are living beings, and occasionally, they make decisions that defy human logic.

We'll take a glance at how to work with certain behavioral issues as we touch on them. I want you to keep in mind, though, that there is no one absolute, fail-proof way to train a horse to do or not do something. Just as people learn in different ways, each horse will respond to different "asks" −or training requests that we make− in different ways. I very much do not want anyone to get hurt or do something that is outside of their comfort zone or realm of knowledge. That can make matters even worse.

Instead, know that working with a professional is a great option for those times when your horse's issues are beyond your training ability. Honesty and humility are important qualities to practice when working with beings as large and powerful as horses. If you are "overhorsed," as we call it, you may make decisions based on your own dangerous instincts. Instead of trying to suffer through this type of situation, it's a smart idea to contact a professional.

Of course, there are plenty of questionable professionals in this world. To help you navigate the world of equine professionals such as trainers, behaviorists, and handlers, I've included a brief discussion regarding some of the many training debates that persist in the equine world. My goal is not to persuade you to take a side, or to change your mind. I simply wish to present all perspectives, as well as common arguments for and against each approach. Therefore, don't think of this book as an endorsement for any particular training method or approach−it's just your horse buddy Meredith telling you about some of the things you might want to think about when considering training for your horse.

Let's start by looking at how good manners are defined so you have a clearer idea of what you should expect from your equine companion. We'll then observe and analyze what your hooved beast is currently doing to determine the best way to get on the same page. As with each of my books, a Resources section will round things up with websites where you can learn more about many of the topics discussed.

With all that said, get ready to dive into what makes an equine good citizen, and how a horse or pony earns such a designation!

Chapter One

What Are Equine Good Manners?

When we think of "good manners," we think of things like saying "please" and "thank you," or actions such as holding a door open for a person who has their hands full. We do not (and should not) expect these types of manners from horses. They don't have the linguistic capability to speak English, and they lack thumbs, so operating doorknobs is a challenge for them.

For the most part, equine good manners boil down to acting in a rational, minimally dangerous manner. There are different ways in which they can demonstrate this preferred behavior, as well. When a horse generally manages to exist peacefully in a stall without damaging itself or the barn, we say that they have "good stall manners." When a horse is being handled by someone, such as being led down the barn aisleway, groomed, or tacked up, without incident, we say that the horse has "good ground manners". When you are able to take your horse into situations where they may encounter other horses, dogs, humans, children, unfamiliar objects, plastic bags, or a ringtone they may not have heard before, and no one cries, we say a horse is "easy to handle."

When a horse is difficult to handle, there is often a combination of factors at play. In most cases, the horse has simply not been desensitized to a particular object or situation. As far as they're concerned, that wheelbarrow in a different place is a horse-eating monster, and that didgeridoo ringtone is the beckoning of the end of days. They have no basis for understanding what it is, they think it's terrifying, and the appropriate reaction is fight or flight.

In addition to being afraid, a horse that demonstrates bad manners and makes choices that are less than satisfactory frequently isn't sure about boundaries or who to trust. Horses either are the leader, or they're desperately looking for the leader so they don't have to make their own decisions. If at all possible, we want the human to be the leader. But, in order for the horse to agree with that decision, they need to know that the leader is competent. In turn, this trust requires communication and understanding, so it's not just as simple as telling a horse what you want it to do in most cases. Think of it more as providing a full persuasive essay, acknowledging the pros and cons of each potential decision, delivered in a language you do not speak fluently.

There may also be some trauma in your horse's past that influences their behavior. Accidents happen, even in the kindest and most compassionate barns. As a result, your horse may be genuinely triggered by certain things.

To prevent them from becoming a danger to themselves and everything around them, it's critical for a horse to have at least semi-halfway-kinda decent manners. I frequently draw comparisons between horses and toddlers because they're on the same wavelength, at least in my experience. They can do things that are compassionate, and rational, and demonstrate advanced problem-solving skills. They can also immediately about-face and have an emotional meltdown about something that you would personally categorize as insignificant.

For example, returning readers are likely familiar with my thoroughbred gelding, Red, and quarter horse mare, Belle. Red made a horrible racehorse and a less-than-ideal children's horse, but over time, we've built a fantastic relationship. He's served as a therapy horse for dozens of humans and horses alike. However, he is still very much a horse. I have seen him stand perfectly still while a small child has a tantrum at his feet, but I have also watched him throw his own tantrum because he didn't want to cross a small mud puddle in his favorite pasture.

Toddlers and horses have a similar capacity for understanding what it means to have good manners, too. They may not completely understand the whys and wherefores, but they grasp the idea that if you tell them it's ok to do something, it's probably ok. They also understand what "no" means, and they'll cheerfully use it in response to your requests, too. Toddlers and horses also have a proclivity towards honesty even, and sometimes especially, when you don't necessarily want them to be quite so upfront. Red used to pin his ears at a vet he didn't like very much, and while I understood, I really wished he would be a little better at concealing his opinions!

You may be wondering whether your horse falls more into the category of "naughty" or "nice" when it comes to manners. Most horses are a combination of both, so don't feel bad if you can think of some "yes, but..." scenarios involving a time your horse was particularly heinous. That happens to even the most staunchly obedient equine citizens, so fear not. "Generally nice" is often a good target for most horses, though we can always aim higher and work towards improvement.

Let's take a look at some of the more common situations in which a horse's manners are most important, for the sake of everyone–and everything–around them.

Chapter 1: Stall Manners

You may have also heard of stall manners as "stable manners" or "barn behavior." Each of these terms is used to describe how a horse acts when it's indoors. Though "stall," "stable," and "barn" are all specific types of structures, these terms are often used interchangeably. Regardless of the semantics, stable manners refer to how a horse behaves regarding its surroundings indoors.

To determine whether your horse is a good citizen or a borderline hooligan, as yourself a few questions about your horse's general behavior. When locked in a stall, do they stand there patiently, or whiny and pace inconsolably? When other horses walk past the stall, does your horse bite at the walls and pin their ears, or have no noticeable reaction? When it's time to clean your horse's stall, do they casually sniff your hair or take a nap in the corner, or do they require a three-person moving team to safely transport them to another stall or paddock?

Your horse may also exhibit one of many inappropriate stall behaviors. We reviewed these topics in detail in my book *Why Does My Horse Act Like This: Understanding Equine Behavior in your new Horse*, so I don't want to become too repetitive, but some horses have developed bad habits as a reaction to stress, pain, or behavioral issues. Horses who crib, chew, weave, stall walk, and dig aren't necessarily being ill-mannered in their destruction of property and acts of self-endangerment, but these behaviors are often categorized as bad manners. They are not encouraged, and it's best to dig deep to discover why your horse continues to do these things so that you can help them break these habits.

In our ideal human mind, a horse would stand in its stall as long as we needed them to. They would cleverly deposit waste in a corner that's easy to reach. They would ring a bell when their water bucket needed attention, and they would never, ever poo in their buckets just moments after we finished scrubbing and refilling them. They would keep their hay neatly piled and put a tidy stack of the bits they didn't want to eat next to the door for easy disposal. They'd whinny happily at all of their neighbors, wait patiently for feeding time, and would never chew on anything, kick at the walls, or drag things from the aisleway into their stalls to destroy.

Our ideal human mind, however, has nothing to do with the instincts and capabilities of modern horses. Horses wander around in their stalls, tracking their waste wherever they go. They slobber up a mess in their water buckets, throw hay everywhere, and more or less give the place the full "rock star trashes a hotel room," treatment. Can a horse be neat and tidy and mild-mannered when locked in a stall full-time? Sure. Just don't expect it.

In your ideal human mind, a horse standing in a stall is no big deal. Heck, you'd probably love to have nothing better to do than stand in a box and eat all day. On the surface, it sounds like a pretty good gig. But try to reverse your perspective and think about it from the point of view of a horse.

Yes, your horse stands there all day and does nothing but eat. But running through their fuzzy head are instincts that tell them to move more, eat more, and socialize more. Horses are genetically predisposed to roam in herds, live in the company of their friends and family, and eat constantly. The biology of horses is such that they need mental stimulation, physical exercise, and an unbelievable amount of roughage to keep them happy.

Stall manners can be taught, and bad stall habits can be curbed, but you'll want to start with a happy horse. Just as a toddler isn't particularly interested in learning about the alphabet when they've just been denied their favorite sweet, a horse who is unhappily fighting his instincts for movement and grazing isn't going to be super receptive to new information. If your horse is currently battling ulcers, they may not be interested in what you have to say about not kicking the door every time their nemesis walks down the aisleway. Obviously, if you are in an emergency situation, that goes out the window, but timing is key when it comes to modifying equine behavior.

Everyone has their own unique version of what they consider good stall manners because everyone's barn situation is a little different. For example, if you don't have stalls, but rather a large communal run-in, you would probably like it if you could walk outside, approach your horse, and put a halter on them. If you have your horse in a traditional stall, you might find it pretty satisfactory if anyone could walk into your horse's stall to clean, feed, check the water bucket, and make sure your horse is doing well. In some barns, it's customary to groom and tack up your horse in their stall, which means you'd probably love it even more if your horse would stand still and not try to escape the stall when the door is open.

Before you start coming up with a training or discipline plan to work all the weird barn habits out of your horse, pause for a moment and prioritize. Many of us have an innate urge to correct bad behavior *right now, with no exceptions!* There may be an extra sense of urgency if you are boarding your horse at another person's property because your horse is being a pest and/or dangerous and/or destructive. Now you're worried about your horse causing problems as well as being held liable for damages, and to top it all off, you might get kicked out of your barn if what your horse did was totally egregious!

No one wants to be the parent of the child lying on the floor screaming their head off in the local supermarket during peak hours. Similarly, no one wants to be the person whose horse ate the entire fence or the person whose horse dragged all of the freshly washed blankets into the stall and covered them in manure. Getting a call from a barn manager or owner informing me that my horse has been naughty is an incredibly embarrassing experience–trust me! I once had a horse who managed to do something fascinating on a near-weekly basis. Each time I got a call, I wanted to sell the horse, hide under a rock, and not think about anything horse-related, no matter how tangential.

Do not do this. Unless you have been strategically planning for some time to sell your horse and turn into a hermit, it is far simpler to apologize, take pictures of everything, document what happened, pay for anything that is legally your responsibility, and work with your horse to help them make better choices. While that does feel like a lot, selling a horse with a reputation for poor stable manners is in itself an extraordinary feat And that's *before* finding the right mountain or deep cave to hide from society for the rest of your life. So skip the real estate hunt. Stay calm. Stay rational. Take care of the horse.

Instead of fleeing town in the dead of night, it's time to start paying very close attention to everything your horse does– the good, the bad, and the inexplicable. Compare what they actually do to what you want and need them to do. Consider how they act when you:

- Enter their stall

- Approach them from a variety of angles

- Move their water bucket or attempt to fill it with a hose

- Attempt to put a halter on in their stall

- Enter with food

- Walk past their stall with and without another horse

- Stick your fingers in their stall (this is especially important if you are boarding at a facility where children are present)

- Stand outside their stall and talk to someone

- Bring a pitchfork and muck bucket into their stall while they're in it

If you have never noticed anything unusual when doing these things with your horse, then you can rest assured that your horse already has pretty good stall manners. But, if your horse becomes aggressive or agitated when these things happen, you might have a few concerns to address.

Before we get to the next steps, though, let's continue to look at all of the interesting ways in which horses can choose to misbehave!

Chapter 2: When You Handle Your Horse

When you're spending time with your horse, what are you typically doing? Many of us "old-timers" go into a bit of a fugue state and have to really stop to consider the actual actions we take when we're at the barn.

If I really think about it, my pattern typically looks something like this:

- Walk up to Red or Belle's stall

- Greet them

- Grab their halter from the front of the stall

- Enter the stall and shut (but don't lock) the door behind me

- Say mushy things about how cute they are and how much I love them

- Put their halter on

- Lead them out of their stall by their halter to the cross ties (don't do this–a lead rope is a much safer and effective way to lead your horse)

- Clip the cross ties onto the halter rings

- Wander into the tack room and pull out my saddle, pads, girth, bridle, and helmet, which I stack on a rack in the aisleway piece by piece as I find them in the crowded tack room

- Groom the horse, including a good curry, body brushing, and hoof picking

- Tack them up, probably very slowly because I enjoy having time to talk to the other folks in my barn

- Walk the horse back down the aisle, past their stall, into the arena

- Fidget and fuss with the girth, stirrup leathers, saddle position, helmet straps, and gloves

- Mount up

- Make final equipment adjustments

- *Finally,* start working

It's entirely forgivable if you stopped really absorbing the steps midway through because it gets boring. I understand why my horses zone out while I'm getting ready for our rides. They have to stand patiently for a significant amount of time, doing absolutely nothing while I'm completely absorbed in my own tasks.

My Quarter Horse mare, Belle, stands completely still through the whole process because that's how she was trained as a youngster. Red, on the other hand, will fidget. As a former racehorse, he wasn't taught much about standing still for anything–many times, track horses are groomed long before a race, then saddled up on the move so they can keep their muscles warmed up for the burst of speed needed for a race.

When Red first came into my life, he lived at a barn where there were no crossties. Horses were either tacked up in stalls or ground-tied next to the area where we kept our equipment (it wasn't so much a "tack room" as a "tack space"). So, we worked at it for a while, and Red learned to ground tie rather nicely. Next, I worked on getting him to continue ground tying even when I started to pull out exciting things like saddle pads and girths. Eventually, we got a pretty good routine down, but I've never been able to convince him to stand completely still as Belle does. He has arthritis, after all, and as a fellow sufferer, I can't imagine standing still feeling very good to him. So I let him move a bit, shift his weight, and get comfortable while I talk to my trainer about something completely irrelevant for far too long.

I have, however, taught him words like "scootch," which means take a step sideways, "bootch," which is his cue to move his hindquarters away from me, "step," which is a request to take a step forward, and "back," which is a step backward. If his wiggling positions him at an angle I don't appreciate, I can easily guide him back to where I need him with a few cues.

Assessing your horse's barn manners means seriously considering how you need your horse to behave indoors. Deciding whether or not your horse is well-mannered when you handle them depends on what you ask them to do, and how much time and effort it takes to get the desired result.

Ask yourself:

- Can I easily catch my horse? Can I just walk up to them wherever they are and put their halter and lead rope on their head?

- When I try to lead my horse out of their stall/pasture, how much resistance do they give me?

- How hard do I need to work to get my horse to walk shoulder-to-shoulder with me? Do I have to drag them behind me, or am I running to catch up?

- When I'm leading my horse, how many feet do they typically have on the ground at any given time? Do I need a spotter to clear a path in front of or behind me?

- What's the most exciting thing that has happened to us while grooming or tacking up? Was it my horse's fault?

- Do people try very hard to not share an arena when I'm working my horse?

- If I had to answer the phone or go to the bathroom urgently while tacking up my horse, would there be imminent danger?

- Are people actively afraid of my horse?

- Am I actively afraid of my horse?

A horse with bad ground manners is scary and dangerous. Whether your horse is being simply contrary or is truly in some stage of "fight or flight" whenever you interact with them, there are too many things that can go wrong to allow this behavior to continue. As a responsible horse owner, you want to be able to interact with your horse safely every time. Accidents will happen, of course, but a horse who knows how to make good choices will often be better prepared to deal with mishaps.

Red is another great example of this. While racehorses aren't necessarily taught to tie while they're on the track, they are exposed to a truly mind-blowing array of traditionally scary things. People are often going in and out of their stalls at strange times. They do something different every day when they go to work. They see a seemingly endless parade of strange faces and places as they travel from track to track. A new wheelbarrow parked in the aisleway for the first time is nothing. A tractor rolling by while you're working? What–are they supposed to yield to you? Goats? They make great buddies! A lot of former racehorses take a lot in stride because they've likely seen it at the track.

Of course, that's not to say that only racehorses can be unbothered by their surroundings, or that all former racehorses are unflappable. All horses spook, but they all have different triggers, and it's important to know what is and is not a problem for them. Red demonstrated this to me early in our relationship.

While he was dancing and prancing up the aisleway during one of our tacking-up training sessions, he managed to get one leg inside the wheelbarrow, and the other on the wrong side of the handles. Instead of freaking out like I fully expected him to, he paused and calmly extracted himself from the wheelbarrow. Once he had all of his feet on the ground, he shook himself and walked up to me as if to ask, "Hey, did you see that? Pretty smooth, eh?"

A few years later, I worked nearly every day for several months to encourage this same mellow creature to walk across a small creek that crossed the trail system at the barn. By "small creek," I mean that I could stand comfortably with my left foot on one bank and my right foot on the other. It was frequently dry and rarely resembled much more than a puddle. I was never able to convince him to walk across. Not once. He would stand stock still on one side or occasionally put his front feet in the creek, but he would not cross. As a bonus, once he decided he'd had enough of this nonsense, he would bolt suddenly and take himself back to his stall at a dead gallop. I gave up.

As it turns out, I have never actually needed to walk Red through water, but I have led him up and down crowded aisleways, through busy barns, alongside roads, and past a variety of strange objects that he's never seen before. His original trainer taught him some very important stuff by making sure he was aware of different objects that might show up in a barn, like wheelbarrows.

Make sure you prioritize your horse's manners based on what they need to know right now, then add the upgrades as you continue to trust each other and grow. You are responsible for deciding your horse's education program, so make sure you select steps that make sense for the here and now first.

Additionally, it's a really good idea to take this type of training one step at a time and try to start with initial contact first. I've known many horses who are equally difficult to catch in their stall or a field, or have snapped and danced while being tacked up, yet were professional babysitters once their rider was aboard. Many steps were skipped in their training process. While this is one possible shortcut when preparing a horse for the show pen, it isn't ideal for all of the people who may interact with your horse.

This brings us to our next point How does your horse act for other people? It's one thing if they maintain their good behavior when you're around them, but what about when other people interact with your horse? Let's take a look at how things may change when someone else is holding the reins.

Chapter 3: When Others Handle Your Horse

You may be thinking that you can skip this step completely because no one but you handles your horse. As long as you know how to adapt and work with their quirks, things will be fine, right?

For the most part, this is true. You might be willing to compromise on some of the finer points of politeness for the sake of focusing on more pressing issues. As I've noted, you need to be able to prioritize what you intend to teach your horse before you start the educational process. Just like the Billboard Hot 100, this list of priorities will continue to fluctuate and change. The goal is to not introduce too much at once to allow your horse to focus on one major skill at a time. And while this means we may have to calm that inner perfectionist who is looking to solve all of the problems immediately, it gives your horse a fair chance to learn everything well so that they fully understand each concept and can apply this new logic on its own.

It's a great idea to make sure your horse is willing to at least have a new human:

- Hold onto their lead rope without having an emotional meltdown

- Lead them around, regardless of how unfamiliar the area

- Touch their body, face, and feet

- Move around them, including moving equipment, talking, etc

When I've mentioned this in the past, other horse folks largely agree with me. However, I occasionally hear this line: *No one but me ever handles my horse, so why does it matter?*

First and foremost, your veterinarian and farrier would deeply appreciate it if they could examine and work with your horse without fearing for their lives. I realize some people do a majority of their diagnostics, treatment, and hoof trimming on their own, and I certainly don't object to that. But what about that one time when your horse does something truly magical and mysterious to themselves in the field and needs x-rays or stitches? What if you discover your horse needs shoes? What if you become injured and can't take care of your horse's hooves on your own?

These are a lot of "what ifs," and in a perfect world, they'll never happen. But My experience has led me to believe that needing a professional at some point is more or less inevitable. No matter how much you try to contain your horse and its bad manners in your own bubble, you will very likely need to have another person touch your horse at some point in their lives.

In fact, that other person might be a future caretaker of your horse. As much as we want to think that our fuzzy friends will live with us forever and ever, there may come a time when it makes sense for them to live with someone else, either in a lease situation or permanently. Generally speaking, it is easier to find a home for a horse that will allow other human beings to handle them than a horse that is allegedly trained, but won't come out of their stall for anyone but you.

Some horses seem to genuinely not care about who is handling them, as long as they aren't being hassled by this new person. Many horses in lesson stables, boarding barns, and training facilities see a rotating cast of characters each day, including stall cleaners, feeders, trainers, riders, vets, farriers, and other horse owners. As long as someone approaches them calmly and quietly, they're pretty accepting of some basic cues.

Other horses have been traumatized somewhere along the line. Belle is not a huge fan of men who are taller than her head, but our vet has been very patient and kindly working with her to help her accept that he's one of the good guys. I don't know how or what happened, but this is something important to note if she ever leaves my care.

When your horse is uncomfortable with another individual handling them, they may refuse to stand still, and prance in place with their head up. They may try to bite or strike out with their feet to remove the perceived danger from their presence. They may absolutely refuse to move their feet, instead choosing to rear to dodge the cue to walk forward. Horses can conjure up some pretty effective evasion tactics for 1,000-pound creatures, and a lot of these reactions can be very dangerous for the horse and everyone and everything around them.

If your horse refuses to act reasonably when other individuals attempt to exist in their presence or ask them to do simple things like pick up a foot or accept a pat on the neck, it may be time for your horse to attend charm school– like the debutantes of yesteryear– to learn some manners.

It's not easy to find someone willing to play the role of guinea pig in your horse-handling experiments because horses can be scary. You need another person who is at least as skilled as you are in handling horses, who knows about timing and can deliver a cue to prevent absolute chaos. At the same time, it's important for your horse to just roll with it when someone asks them to lead forward the "wrong" way or makes a simple perceived "mistake" in their routine.

Even if you don't distinctly foresee your horse needing to behave for another person, it's a great idea to prepare your beast for the potential of having to behave regardless of who is handling them. As my trainer has told me numerous times, "Don't train a horse for yourself." This means that, when working with a horse to develop good manners and behaviors, it's important to have a horse that knows how to react to *what* you're asking, not the specific way you, personally, ask for it.

If you train a horse to only be handled or ridden by yourself, you are not doing that horse any favors in life. Imagine a toddler who only responds to being told "no" by a certain individual. And one day, that toddler is standing by an open gate on a busy road, alone, and they're scared. I'll end the scene there because I honestly don't want to imagine it, but the point stands.

It may not be your main goal today or tomorrow, but if you're not sure how your horse will act when being handled by others, you might want to bump that experiment up on your priority list until you know for sure.

While you're at it, you might want to look further into how your horse acts and reacts when anyone or anything unfamiliar suddenly appears on their turf.

Chapter 4: General Interaction with People, Animals, and Strange Objects

You may be wondering when your horse is going to encounter other people and animals, and why you should worry. You may also be curious about what constitutes a "strange" object.

For some horses, people are strange objects. People come in different shapes, sizes, personalities, and noise levels. As humans, we acknowledge that each individual of our species is unique. We recognize tall, short, wide, thin, old, and young people as human beings. We recognize people in wheelchairs or strollers, we understand how mobility aids work, and we know that people come in different colors and wear different types of clothing.

Horses also come in different shapes, sizes, personalities, and noise levels. As humans, we will freely admit when a horse intimidates us. You may prefer to work with ponies only. Measuring less than 14.2 hands (or 58 inches) from hoof to withers, ponies are physically smaller than horses, yet often have double the orneriness. Some folks enjoy that. Others prefer working with gentle giant draft horses only. Just like humans, horses come in all sorts of packages, and sometimes, we feel more comfortable handling a specific type of package.

So let's flip that. If we have concerns about the type of horse we work with, why shouldn't horses be equally concerned about the humans they work with? In each case, the preferences aren't dictated by a weird bias or prejudice, but by an understanding of the situation and what could go wrong. A human looks at an 18-hand (72 inches) horse standing with their head raised, nostrils flared, and eye whites showing, and decides whether they can safely handle this horse, given their experience. A horse looks at a child red-faced and crying in the aisleway and decides whether they can safely interact with this being, given their experience. (Just a reminder–the Resources section will include links to general horse information, in case some of these terms are new to you!)

A horse's instincts tell it to assume that anything unfamiliar is very likely dangerous. Therefore, when your horse meets a baby, sees a human in a wheelchair, or hears the weird rustly sound of snow pants for the first time, they may be very concerned. In most cases, however, horses have a pretty good memory for knowing what is human, once they've been properly introduced.

The typical response for a horse who is encountering a new human-related situation is caution. They might refuse to get too close to the new person, instead stretching their long necks to sniff and explore the situation with their lips from what they feel is a safe distance. They might also snort, shake their head, and dance around a bit while they decide if walking up to this new being is a good idea. Most horses can be convinced to drop their apprehension with a few favorite treats, some kind words, and a few minutes to take everything in and process it. Allow them to approach on their own time while using their sense and instincts to suss things out, and many horses will acquiesce to meeting all sorts of new acquaintances–human and non-human.

On the other hand, some horses are far more intimidated by new friends. The most common reaction I've seen among horses who are being introduced to new humans is moving backward suddenly or bolting away from the potential danger. I've seen this type of behavior most often when introducing strollers or other types of child-toting equipment. A person in a wheelchair often looks like a person sitting down, which many horses recognize. They rarely react with interest until the chair actually starts rolling. A child in a stroller, however, comes with all sorts of different smells, sounds, and motions, many of which are completely new to the average horse.

Again, you may be wondering why you need to figure out how well your horse deals with strollers or canes, or snow pants. (That's a real thing, by the way– I once knew a horse who couldn't handle the swishy sound made by snow pants, track pants, or the down jacket I used to wear when doing chores in the winter months.)

Your horse may not have to deal with anyone else right now, but consider the following possible–and not so far-fetched–scenarios:

- Your horse needs to travel to see a new vet, farrier, or trainer

- You decide to move your horse to a barn where other people board their horses

- Your friend moves their horse into your private facility

- You add to your family, such as introducing a new child, spouse, or partner

- You have an accident and need to use crutches or a cane for a bit

- Family comes to visit you

- You join a trail riding group that meets up regularly

- You start attending horse shows or 4H/Pony Club events

- You choose to lease your horse to an individual temporarily

- You sell your horse

- You pass away before your horse

I know some of those are pretty grim, and it's not my intention to bring us all down. However, each of these is a scenario I have seen play out in real life. Having a horse that can not only be handled by other people, as we discussed in the last chapter but who can handle having other people around is beneficial in all of these situations.

The same goes for introducing your horse to other animals. I cannot think of a barn where I have worked or boarded where dogs and cats were not among the menagerie of creatures on-premises. And yet, plenty of horses are terrified of each.

This makes perfect sense, really. Dogs and cats are predators and behave as such. Horses are prey animals, and they are genetically pre-programmed to believe never the twain shall meet. In many situations, the dogs and cats are more terrified of the horses than the horses are of the smaller creatures. Still, today's horses are descended from terrier-sized creatures known as *eohippus*, so a strong sense of caution is very much present whenever horses encounter other barn creatures.

Again, the appropriate reaction is to sniff, snort, back up a little, and take a few moments for each creature to assess the other. Dogs may bark, circle, or play-bow as they work on this big, smelly puzzle. Cats frequently hiss or swat. Some cats have the sense to avoid horses entirely. Other cats will sleep in horse stalls, once they know who their friends are.

Some horses are more "fight" than "flight," and will aggressively attempt to seek out and destroy any smaller critter. I know more than one horse that will stop whatever they're doing to chase a cat. In only one case was this a friendly situation? I once worked with a young former racehorse who was obsessed with cats. Furthermore, the cats were obsessed with him. I found that I had to put the barn cats in the tack room when I was working with this horse because the minute one of his kitty friends entered the arena, he would run over to the cat and let it rub all over his face. Then they'd groom each other, which was just as awkward and difficult as you might expect it to be. Yet they insisted.

While you may not have to worry about dogs or cats in your barn at this particular moment, be aware that they will likely be present at other facilities and showgrounds. Cats in particular are helpful around barns and stable facilities as they help control the population of wild animals who stop by to check out the food and shelter situation. Then again, I know many horses who attack all types of uninvited guests, including rats and raccoons.

Your horse doesn't have to graciously accept all attention from other animals, but it is helpful if they approach them just as they do people– with curiosity and interest. Many horses are generally relaxed about meeting new animals, but the bleat of a goat, the sudden fan of a peacock's tail, or the array of noises made by a donkey may be a cause for concern. Having good manners will enable your horse to make good choices and react safely if they ever have to meet new friends.

Then there's the multitude of weird stuff that horses can potentially encounter in their world. It is impossible to shield horses from weird stuff because it is impossible to predict what a horse will consider "weird." Red, for example, has no problem with a lot of the things I personally find a bit unnerving. Those who have read my other books are familiar with his general unflappability, and how fascinating I think it is when he reacts to something. He's had umbrellas open in his face, balloons land on his head, and plastic bags get stuck on his feet. He's stood stock still while teenage boys wrestled under his feet, he's snuggled babies, and he has no problem with wheelchairs, strollers, or those motorized toy cars that kids like to argue over more than actually drive. He's a friend to all he meets. You can put his blanket on upside down, inside out, and backward if you feel like it.

Red is also very concerned with a particular set of work lamps that we keep in the arena during the winter months for those who don't need the full arena lighting. The arena measures 60 feet by 120 feet, so flicking on all of those lights is expensive. The smaller work lights provide plenty of light so folks can walk through the arena to the fields or other parts of the barn. Unfortunately, Red has decided they are evil and must be destroyed. He has pulled them out of their fixtures and destroyed the plugs several times. As I write this book, I'm currently working with him to convince him that these actions are not necessary. Just leave them alone. Progress is slow so far, but he's also very bored at present after having some time off due to frigid weather, so it's not a cut-and-dry training situation.

Nor will it ever be. Whenever you work to desensitize your horse to any specific item, person, or animal, something will go sideways. The garbage truck will pull up loudly. A bicycle will whizz by. The neighbor's dog will start barking. The wind will start blowing, or the temperature might change. This is why we continuously work with our horses to help them maintain equine good citizenship. Something about the situation will always be different, and your horse will have a choice of how to respond. Whether or not your horse registers this situation as dangerous or not, the goal is for them to respond in a way that is not dangerous in itself.

It's ok for your horse to get a little excited about new things. Even the most seasoned show horses tend to get a little perky when they unload from the trailer in a new place. Horses rely on their senses to stay alive, which means they have a lot to take in and process at once. You might feel overwhelmed when you show up at a new place, too. Who do these new faces belong to? What are others like here? New sounds and smells, accompanied by things you've never seen before are bound to be overwhelming, regardless of your species!

On the other hand, it is not ok for your horse to act in a way that is dangerous to you and everyone and everything around you. Your definition of "dangerous" might be a bit different at various points in your life, too. For example, I've known several trainers who greatly dialed back on the shenanigans they were willing to tolerate during their pregnancies.

The best way to ensure that your horse has praise-worthy manners and can handle themselves in a variety of situations is to work with them as much as possible on their manners. This includes desensitizing them to different people, animals, objects, and places.

This doesn't necessarily have to be a Great Big Training Extravaganza, either. In many cases, I've had the opportunity to introduce a horse to a new person or thing just because it's there. One time, a barn owner had gotten a new tarp, and she was airing it over the fence line. I immediately took Red over there so he could meet the tarp. A new hose, wheelbarrow, or even a differently-shaped feed bucket can become a fascinating learning experience, depending on what your horse has decided is threatening.

The goal is to always come into a situation expecting the best but anticipating the worst. That means knowing the possible reactions your horse might have while remaining calm and confident that this will be a non-issue. There's an old saying that horses can "smell fear," but I'm not sure that it's so much an odor or pheromone that they recognize, as much as the frozen, big-eyed, non-committal, shaky way we often approach things when we're not sure what's going to happen next. Is the big horse going to walk past the scary plastic bag, or are we all going to get stitches tonight? There's no guarantee, and that can be intimidating for both horse and human.

When someone has more horse issues than they have solutions, we say they're "overhorsed." If you are overhorsed, it's a great idea to invoke the expertise of a professional. Whether you have a trainer come to you, drop your horse off at the trainer, or video chat with a trainer, you are still taking a very important step in helping your horse become an equine good citizen.

But here's the hard part. As I've mentioned several times, you'll need to do several challenging things simultaneously:

- Pay attention to your horse's bad behavior

- Determine if it's caused by something other than naughtiness

- Prioritize how essential it is to deal with this behavior

- Attempt to not obsess over the potential for disaster

- Keep your cool and move to a remote location

- Consider the most important situations to address with your horse

- Adjust as needed because your horse will probably also get an abscess or throw a shoe, or some other aspect of your life will need your attention for a week or so

It's going to be a process. Unless you are a professional or can afford a professional to work with your horse every single day until all of their issues are sorted, it's going to be a long, arduous, ridiculous, frustrating process. You'll take one step forward, ten steps back, and show up on an entirely different path two days later.

But if we're being honest here, isn't that how our learning process goes, too? Did you learn how fractions work overnight? Probably not, but eventually, you got the concept of what "half" of something is, as well as the symbol: "1/2". It took a while for the words and symbols and ideas to have meaning, but once they did, you likely became a professional at precisely splitting any delicious food item in the school cafeteria.

Learning is rarely linear, which is why I mention that list of priorities changes frequently. This is understandably intimidating. But your goal is not to find perfection in training your horse but to find moments in which you and your horse sync up and understand each other perfectly. With practice, these moments will get longer and longer. You and your horse will always have a miscommunication here or an attitude-driven disagreement there because you are both living beings. But working on politeness, understanding, and good manners from the ground up can help you remain safe and regain clear communication quickly.

Now that you have a few things to look for and think about, let's start considering the next steps for helping your horse understand good manners. First, you'll need to really pay attention to your horse, along with your own actions and reactions, so that you can address the situation accurately and appropriately, or more specifically, without things escalating.

It's time to observe and analyze the bad-mannered horse, as well as the well-intentioned human who hopes to turn that naughtiness around.

Chapter Two

What Behaviors Are You Observing?

I 've had this conversation many times:

Person: My horse is a jerk.

Me: Oh really? What are they doing?

Person: They're just nasty.

Me: Like biting you?

Person: No, just like being mean.

Me: When?

Person: I don't know, like all the time.

Me: What are you doing when they do this?

Person: Nothing! I'm just standing there!

Every single time, I give them a moment, then ask a very important question:

So, what am I supposed to do?

I don't say it to be a smart aleck, though I do usually ask with a sense of humor and empathy. But the question stands. You've just shared with me that your horse is a mean, nasty jerk when you are standing somewhere in their presence.

We can only change a situation once we've recognized our current situation and decided what needs to be changed. I don't know how to tell a horse not to be a jerk. I know how to correct a horse who is biting, train a horse to stand tied patiently, and teach a horse that its winter blanket is not going to eat them, but I don't know how to convince a horse not to be mean. This is extra true when I have no context about when or how the horse is being "nasty."

I don't expect new horse people to use advanced veterinary terminology when describing whatever their horse is doing. But to train a horse, any professional needs to know what the horse is doing, what you would prefer it does instead, and how you're currently responding to the naughtiness.

There are many other factors to take into account when attempting to describe, diagnose, understand, and correct bad behavior, most of which I hinted at in the last section. Whenever you're experiencing equine naughtiness, it's important to also consider:

- Your horse's recent health changes

- Your recent health changes

- Weather changes

- Stabling changes

- Routine changes

- Feed changes

- Turnout changes

- The horse's background/training/experience

- Your background/training/experience

- The horse's past trauma

- Your past trauma

- What you're currently working on in other areas

- What's going on around you

- Where you're working

- How important changing this behavior is to you

- How stressed your horse is about this behavior

- How stressed you are about this behavior

Generally speaking, none of this is in your control. Most changes that are within our control occur not because we're feeling bored and want to change things up, but because a series of circumstances have conspired against us. It's usually not possible for us to help our horses understand why these things should make sense to them.

Then again, very little of what might cause a horse to engage their instincts and behave against their training makes sense. Therefore, we need to take a closer look at those things that we can control, such as identifying the behavior, reacting, and trying to stop it.

Let's dig in a little more into these areas to help suss out the full picture of your horse's misbehavior.

Chapter 1: What Does Your Horse Do That You Don't Like?

This is the easiest question of them all, but it's not as simple as it may appear. Horses are more creative than we give them credit for. While it would be great if our issues were cut-and-dry, like "My horse bites anyone who is wearing a blue hat," it's usually more, "My farrier wore a blue hat the other day, and my horse bit him, so then my farrier yelled at my horse, and the horse got all startled and started dancing in the aisleway but then slipped on the aisle footing and snapped the cross ties, and then my farrier's cart knocked over, so my horse bolted and ran across the arena while there was a lesson going on, and now I haven't been able to coax them out of their stall in three days. Also, my trainer has a price on my head because my horse knocked a little girl off her pony and her mother pulled her out of the lesson program."

If you're wondering if that really happened, the answer is yes, and I still feel terrible about it. The point is, however, that horses frequently misbehave in situational ways, rather than by doing one naughty thing. Even if the behavior seems straightforward– "my horse kicks his stall walls when another horse is led past his stall," there's likely a little more to it than that.

It's helpful for everyone involved if you carefully observe your horse's behavior from beginning to end. For example, if they seem to lose their sense of reason every time they walk down the aisleway of your barn, consider the scene and any potential triggers. What objects are present? Is the sun shining off of anything strange? Does the horse get weird when it passes a particular spot or stall? Are there other horses present? Are there other people or animals present? Does it happen any time of day, or only at certain hours? There are so many strange and unusual factors that can inspire behavioral issues in horses that it's a good idea to really pay attention not only to the priority issue of your horse freaking out but to the full scene and action of the event.

The human brain tends to have a hard time processing a potentially traumatic event like a large horse violently spooking in an aisleway while remembering all of the details in minutiae, so don't feel bad if you can't remember whether Jennifer was standing by Patch's stall, or Hillary was pushing the wheelbarrow past Henry in the cross ties. But knowing that there were two people, one wheely, a squeaky object, and another horse involved can help you narrow down the options of what is offending your horse.

To illustrate, let's revisit the concept of a horse who kicks its stall wall when other horses are being led past. So far, so good. You're able to determine a definite stimulus for your horse's behavior. But try asking yourself more questions about the scenario. Does your horse kick every time a horse is led past? If the answer is yes, then congratulations! You've got a very clear situation!

In many cases, however, there's far more to it. Observation is key to helping unlock the secrets of why your horse is being so naughty. Consider the full situation, rather than the individual behaviors. It may be that your horse kicks when other horses are being led past their stall, but only when horses are being led past their stall in the morning as they're being turned out for a few hours. Then, when those horses are brought back inside, your horse paces and stall walks. And perhaps your horse was previously turned out in the morning, but for any number of reasons, they're now part of the afternoon turnout herd.

Your horse is reacting to the fact that they're expecting to follow a routine, but that routine has been disturbed. That doesn't mean that the kicking behavior is appropriate, but it now tells you what problem you're trying to solve, rather than wishing it was possible to temporarily glue a horse's feet to the floor.

When it comes to deciding what behavior you want to modify, you first have to figure out what that behavior is. In this example, we want to stop the kicking, but most importantly, we want to stop the horse from explosively sharing its feedback regarding the turnout schedule changes. If your horse is that unhappy about something, it'll find new ways to be reactive, even if you stop the initial behavior. Gluing your horse's hooves to the floor would– hypothetically– stop the kicking, but there's a good chance your horse would then find a new way to express their displeasure.

This is equally true of situations where the behavior is more explosive and sudden. I once knew–and most long-time equestrians have once known–a horse who was just fine until she wasn't. I was once commissioned to hold this type of horse for the farrier. Her owner was out of town, and as the tallest, youngest, and strongest person in the barn, I was given the honor. Things started out just fine. The horse was never exactly relaxed, but she stood still with me at the end of the lead rope. The first hoof was rebalanced, reshod, and reshaped with no problem. Then, as the farrier was rasping the second hoof, something changed. She started to get dancy and distracted. Every sound would be a reason for concern. Her eyes became wider and wider, and her nostrils flared as her breath grew more rapid. It was at this point that she departed reality, heading straight up into the air on her hind legs.

This was, sadly, typical behavior for her any time she was asked to stand still for long periods of time. Farriers have a very delicate job of getting angles and pressure just right for a horse's anatomy and stride, so they tend to make many small adjustments to ensure the best performance and most comfortable for each individual horse. Standing still for that long simply wasn't in this horse's wheelhouse.

The worst part was that for days after having her feet done, she would prance, kick, and nip at anyone who tried to touch her feet because she associated picking up her feet with the "torture" of standing still. Horses typically have the farrier reshape and rebalance their hooves every 6-8 weeks, so it felt like she was just becoming herself again when it would be time for another round.

There were three possible solutions here:

1. Tranquilize her every time someone needed to touch her feet

2. Throw a chain around her lip and have two people wrestle her down every time she tried to go up

3. Make sure she was adequately fed and exercised as much as possible before the farrier arrived, combined with taking multiple breaks to help her reset her head

Each plan has merit and challenges, so let's discuss in more detail:

Plan 1: On one hand, tranquilizing her means she'd be calm and sedate through the entire process. For the most part, sedation is a standard veterinary process with minimal risks.

On the other hand, many types of sedation require a veterinarian to be on-premises. Furthermore, having her sedated each time her feet are cleaned– daily– means she would be eternally out of it.

Plan 2: Twitches and lip chains are often considered cruel, due to the way they pinch the horse's large top lip and twist around, tightening around the flesh. There are many wrong ways to do this, but if done right, a lip chain can actually calm a horse by releasing endorphins. The idea is to twist to the point where the horse is naturally non-resistant, then release so they can get lost in the sauce for a few.

However, many people take this approach with aggression and try to fight a resisting horse blow-by-blow. No matter how superhumanly strong your anger, adrenaline, and emotions make you in the heat of the moment, reflect back to the horsepower example I gave in the introduction. Your horse will either win this fight or be prepared to die trying.

Plan 3: This is the most humane plan, obviously. It takes into consideration the real situation behind the behaviors–the horse is likely bored out of her mind standing in one spot for so long, so she's looking for interesting things to do. Then, once she's at the end of her mental and emotional tether, she acts out.

The problem with this method is that it could potentially take all day. And while I constantly preach the whole "it will take as long as it takes" rhetoric, your farrier does not care about training your horse. Your farrier wants to get through the day without being stepped on, to be paid fairly for each horse, and to go home to lie on their heating pad or ice pack for 2-3 hours. If you want your farrier to stick around all day while you take as many breaks as necessary to wind your horse down to have their feet touched, you'd best plan on paying them accordingly.

Ultimately, we ended up doing a little bit of all three at first. The horse was first lunged until she was content and relaxed. Then she ate her breakfast with a vet-approved dose of acepromazine in it. Once she seemed a little more chilled out than usual, two people would accompany her to the farrier–one to hold the lead rope, and the other to administer a lip chain as needed. When the horse started getting fussy during the visit, she was given a break to walk up and down the aisle. When she reared up, she was backed rapidly into the arena while her regular handler (taller and more experienced than I) would administer discipline. For this horse, that included sharp, tight jerks on the lead rope until she brought "all four to the floor" and relaxed through her neck.

But what about letting the lesson students touch their feet? It turns out, once the horse was no longer thoroughly traumatized by the process of standing still, she wasn't triggered as much by people touching her feet. Other than making sure only experienced riders handled her immediately following a farrier visit, we didn't need to tip-toe around her anymore, pun intended.

This was not accomplished in one visit, of course. All told I'd say it was about a full year of following this type of program before everyone–the horse, the farrier, and the two handlers–felt comfortable with this routine. And though the horse has long passed through my life to another barn, I would not be surprised if the routine remains in place.

I tell this story to illustrate my meaning when I ask what your horse is doing that you don't like. You could say "rearing for the farrier," but that wasn't the issue here, was it? The real issue was a horse who was disinclined to stand still for long periods.

Furthermore, the answer wasn't "fix it." Instead, we did our best to make the horse comfortable with the process, so that everyone involved could remain safe. You can't force an animal the size of a horse to do something perfectly every single time. In fact, one might even argue that you can't force any animal to do something perfectly every single time. Can you make it through a pedicure silently, without shifting in your seat or letting your attention wander?

Instead, we helped the horse deal with the situation in the safest way possible. Do I love the fact that this plan included sedatives and lip chains? Yes and no. On one hand, my inner idealist wishes the horse could have been coaxed to accept and understand. On the other hand, regular farrier work and safety are equally necessary. The goal was to accomplish both without traumatizing the horse, and I think we achieved that.

I've gone a little bit past the starting point here with this example, but I wanted to explain how important recognizing the true nature of a horse's "bad" behavior can be. In some cases, yes, a quick tug on a lead rope or tap on the shoulder with a riding crop will be enough to return the horse to its thinking brain. In others, though, you may find yourself doing a lot of observational research, and trying out a lot of different angles to approach and address the true behavior with empathy and kindness.

Chapter 2: How Are You Reacting?

This question is a true test of one's humility because honesty is required. Quite frequently, when a horse starts misbehaving and acting out of instinct instead of intelligence, we humans follow suit. When the large, unpredictable beast starts acting as big and dangerous as we know it is, we stop thinking about analyzing and resolving situational behavior, and we do whatever it takes to save ourselves.

This may include doing things we've been told never to do, such as:

- Letting go of the lead rope or lunge line

- Running

- Curling into the fetal position with our arms over our heads

- Screaming

These are all things we're taught not to do during our first interaction with a horse, and yet it is our instinct to do all of them, simultaneously, when things get scary.

I would like to take this moment to humble myself by publicly admitting that I have done all of these. In fact, I have done some of them on purpose. Let's take them one by one to examine the merits and challenges.

Letting Go: The ramifications of this one are pretty obvious. When you let go of a horse, you no longer have any control over them. They will go where their currently overwhelmed brains take them.

However, if you are currently attached to a horse by a six-foot cotton/poly blend rope, and that horse is getting ready to move at great speed, you should definitely let go, or risk being pulled by the horse. If you are currently in a cart or sleigh, that might be fun or festive, but when you're standing in a busy barn aisleway, it is significantly less jolly.

Running: Horses are prey animals, so something running towards them is often interpreted as a potential predator. They may kick or nip to rid themselves of the attacker. If something is running away from them, they frequently wonder why the herd is going in that direction and try to join.

But if you are in an area in which a horse is going ballistic, and you are not directly involved in mitigating the situation, get out. Rapidly. Even at a run if you must. This is not one of those instances where we form a protective crowd around the panicked animal because that will intensify the situation.

Protective Positioning: Riding horses has helped me appreciate how much humans love the fetal position. Whenever we get overwhelmed, our bodies react by curling our skeletons around our vital organs. Even sitting astride a horse, the human body tends to curl up when it feels unstable. The act of riding involves the relaxation and control of every muscle group, though, so this position is impractical for riding purposes.

On the ground, however, it's absolutely ok to get small to avoid a tantruming horse. If you're not in a position to handle the situation, get as far out of it as possible and protect yourself. That might mean crouching in the corner of a wash rack or trying to make yourself invisible in a trailer. Protect yourself, always. If you need to wear a helmet, gloves, and a protective body vest while handling your horse when they're working through bad behavior, by all means, do!

Screaming: Horses do not care for loud, sudden noises– again, due to their prey animal status. They are easily startled, and their reaction to loud, sudden noises might be exactly what you're trying to work on, behaviorally speaking.

Sometimes, however, we can take advantage of a horse being easily startled by loud, sudden noises to distract them from whatever other terrible behavior they're demonstrating. Just like humans, horses can be trained to recognize "cease and desist" noises, such as roaring "QUIT!" or "NO!" or "BAD!" in a loud, assertive tone. One of my trainer friends calls it her "Horse Mom Voice," while another calls it his "Yes, Sir Voice." I'm not saying it's wise to horror-film holler, but loud voice commands can be used effectively to stop a horse from getting too deep into their instincts and emotions.

You've also likely heard that horses and other animals can "smell fear" or "sense nervousness." There is some truth to that. Horses communicate through body language, so they're frequently scanning our own actions to get a feel for how they should react. If there's a loud, sudden noise and you jump nervously, chances are high that your horse is going to also react. However, if there's a loud, sudden noise, and you have absolutely no reaction whatsoever, your horse is more likely to assume that everything is perfectly fine.

Horses are also not big fans of physical punishment. Yes, absolutely, there are times when a well-placed chain or whip can deliver an important and humane message, but that message should ultimately be, "Pull your brain together, Fluffy, and work with me here!" If you approach a horse with these tools from a standpoint of punishment for their behaviors, they may not be as understanding.

We'll get more into conditioning and "reward versus punishment" shortly, but for now, remember that horses are instinct-based creatures. When something unpleasant happens to them, their ultimate goal is to get out of that situation. Approaching bad behavior with anger and resentment is far more likely to escalate the dangerous actions of both humans and beasts.

When your horse starts doing whatever it is that you want them to stop doing, pay close attention to what you're doing as a reaction. Is it possible that what you're doing isn't effective at all, or potentially counter-effective? If your horse pulls backward on the lead rope, and the first thing you do is let go time after time, you'll eventually teach your horse a nifty way to get away from you, and your horse will have taught you a new way to fear them.

It may also be that what you're doing is escalating things. This may not be through intentional punishment, but the way you react may actually cause the horse to become more agitated or afraid. Horses look to their herd leaders for cues on how to act when things aren't right, and if you're lying on the floor crying, your horse may assume things are really, really bad.

And yet, looping back around to the beginning of this chapter, there are situations where letting go and lying on the floor might not just be your instinct, but your best choice. This is why horse training is so complicated.

Much like Kenny Rogers in *The Gambler*, you, "gotta know when to hold 'em and know when to fold 'em." This takes a lot of practice and many mistakes, as any professional can attest. As I've said before and shall continue to say, if you are over-horsed, it is absolutely appropriate to call in a professional. Just make sure you're ready, to be honest with them when they ask how you act when your horse is being naughty!

Chapter 3: What Have You Tried?

At first, this may seem like an identical question to "How are you reacting." After all, the way you react is what you've tried, right?

Without arguing over semantics, I'd like to emphasize the word "tried." This is to indicate that you actually put thought and physical effort into correcting your horse's behavior, rather than letting your own instincts take over.

At the same time, if your instinct is to slap your horse in the face when it tries to bite you, that's important information for any and all parties involved in solving this riddle. And please note that I'm not judging you for this counterstrike in the least. For many of us, it's quite natural to swat at something approaching our personal space as a protective measure. In most cases, the spontaneous blow a human can administer to a horse in this situation is minimal compared to the damage the horse was about to impart. And, in quite a few cases, it's all that's needed to convince the horse to reconsider that particular behavior.

That's not to say I'm advocating for beating your horse in the face. In fact, I urge you not to beat your horse at all, ever. Instead, I'm saying that it is important to pay attention to both your reactions and actions and the role they play in diminishing or escalating a horse's behavior.

Furthermore, I'd like to make a distinction between a bump or nudge and a slap or punch. The former is setting a type of physical boundary– "You may not enter this zone or continue this nonsense."

The latter is actual abuse, likely stemming from an explosive combination of emotions including but not limited to frustration, anger, regret, confusion, fear, blind rage, or that feeling you get when you don't know exactly the right thing to do at the right time. The velocity with which a bump and a slap are delivered also varies greatly, as does the location of delivery. Swatting your horse on the rump is exactly as effective as swatting a toddler on the rump– they may act as if this is the most sadistic injustice they have ever experienced, or they may completely ignore you.

However, the act of setting a physical boundary with a large body part is a significant communication strategy between horses. Nipping, swinging your hindquarters into an offending party's face, and pinning the ears back while flaring the nostrils and showing the whites of the eyes are all common ways horses tell each other, "Back off! I mean it! Right now!" Swatting, bumping, nudging, and pushing your horse are all similar to the equine response of "Hey! Stop being a jerk!" The difference between communicating with your horse in equine body language and straight-up beating your horse boils down to education, duration, and intent.

Let's look at these concepts in a little more detail:

- **Education**: By this, I mean how educated are you in this method of behavior modification? The difference between teaching and trauma lies in delivering your response in a balanced, calm, reinforcing manner, which in turn requires perfect timing. This can be daunting even to seasoned professionals. Mistakes will be made, and there are a lot of "right choice/right time" situations that have the potential to escalate into a disaster. To properly "reform" a horse's naughty behavior, it's important that you feel skilled and confident enough to conduct their training.

- **Duration**: Making physical contact with your horse in any manner should last seconds, not minutes. When we're riding, we'll kick or bump our horses with the heel of our foot to urge them to go forward. We do not raise our legs to hip height and repeatedly slam giant spurs into our horses' flanks unless the situation absolutely calls for it. If your "punishment" or "correction" method lasts more than a moment, it very well may be–however unintentionally–escalating the situation. The goal is not to make the horse regret their actions but to understand that they made the wrong decision. You're here to help the horse choose wisely, not be left without a choice.

- **Intent**: Again, you must leave your emotions and ego behind when attempting to train horses. There will be many shiny, glowing moments of success that are quickly overshadowed by your horse doing *exactly* the thing you've been trying to talk to them about. There may be times when you find yourself questioning all of your life decisions up to that exact moment. But you can't let your horse know about it. In many cases, all they are aware of is that some collection of cells in their brain made their whole body do something all at once. And, if they're doing this behavior on purpose, it's likely because they've learned that doing this behavior is advantageous in some way. Again, this is why observing and understanding why this behavior is occurring is so important– if you know what your horse's intention is, you can act with equal intention. Beating your horse in a fit of rage will very likely stop that specific behavior, but it's not a long-term fix. It's the start of an entirely different set of problems. Reacting and acting consciously and purposefully when your horse misbehaves gives you the chance to stop that behavior and help your horse understand what better choices are available.

So, if you are asked by a trainer, barn owner, vet, or concerned party asking, "What have you tried?" the best response is the truth. Either it's working, it hasn't done anything, or it has made things significantly worse. In most cases, having the assistance of experts is the best way to alleviate situations where nothing seems to be working, or things have escalated.

Other things to mention under the umbrella of "what have you tried" include:

- Nothing

- Ignoring the horse when they are misbehaving

- Letting the horse "work it out on their own"

- Immediately returning your horse to their stall/pasture

- Requesting someone else deal with it

- Using any gadgets or gizmos recommended by your horse buddies

- Feeding the horse when they are misbehaving

None of these responses are inherently "wrong," though some horse professionals may wish to persuade you otherwise. I like to believe that we are all doing our best, and though we may make mistakes, it's important to educate ourselves and maintain forward motion and progress in our understanding. So, while someone might emphatically explain that, "doing xxx is the worst possible thing you could ever do for your horse, ever," I encourage you to take that with a grain of salt unless you are admittedly beating your horse in a wanton rage.

By keeping track of all of your reactions and actions regarding your horse's misbehavior, you can better identify the severity and frequency of the problem, as well as note what doesn't work, what works a little bit, and what makes things worse. From there, you can choose a new course of action for both you and the horse to either work through or work around the problem.

Now that we have an acute awareness of the behavior, as well as accountability on our own part as the human involved in these mischievous moments, let's attempt to step inside the horse's mind to get their side of the story.

Chapter Three

What Is Your Horse Trying to Tell You?

From your point of view, what your horse is doing is scary, and you need them to cease and desist immediately. But what's going on from your horse's point of view?

Unfortunately, they can't really tell us what set them off in human words. However, watching your horse's facial expressions, body language, and overall movement can tell us more about what they're experiencing.

It may seem at this point that working with horses involves a lot of observing and understanding. This is correct. We are two parties who share no common language, attempting to communicate about activities that are unnatural to both of us.

Imagine you are in a foreign country for the first time. You recognize some of the words in their language, but certainly not enough to try to string together a sentence. Let's say you're enjoying your visit, strolling along a city street during a patch of drizzle, when a sudden gust of wind blows under your umbrella, carrying it off into a nearby sewer drain. Now what do you do? You certainly have the option to ignore the situation and carry on. You can buy a new umbrella. Or you can try to enlist the help of a resident by explaining your situation. How do you convince a stranger who speaks a different language that your umbrella is in the sewer? Even if you used the right words, they'd likely assume you were joking, mad, or mistaken. It's not a common enough scenario that you'd be able to adequately pantomime while using broken phrases in an unfamiliar language.

Let's rearrange this scenario slightly, and replace the human with a horse. And not only are they not sure why you're telling them there's an umbrella in the sewer, but their very instincts are also telling them that things flying around is a big problem and they need to get out of there right away. You're not going to be able to pantomime with your horse. You don't have the luxury of a phone translation app, either. What can help you in this situation is a general understanding of your horse's physical communication methods.

Not only does a horse's body language help us understand that they're upset in the first place, but frequently, they're attempting to communicate a very specific issue. Let's take a look at some of the ways horses try to explain things to us via facial expressions, overall body language, and how they might be moving their bodies.

Chapter 1: Facial Expressions

When we think of horses, we tend to think of them standing nobly, calmly, and blissfully. We don't often think of horses with eyes rolling, nostrils flared, jaws gaping, and ears pinned tightly against their heads.

Those types of scenes are reserved for heroic battle sculptures and stirring artwork, right?

As is frequently the case, art imitates life, and those dramatic warrior horse expressions do, in fact, exist. However, most horses are a bit more subtle in their day-to-day facial communications, which makes observing and understanding their behavior so interesting and important.

When we talk about a horse's facial expressions, this includes their ears, eyes, nostrils, and mouth. All of these parts of a horse are expected to move at some point in time, so this is not as dire as counting how many times your horse blinks, or every swivel of their ears. Instead, we're looking for remarkable expressions and their connection to different behaviors.

There are a few general guidelines about what a horse's ear position, amount of visible eye white, and nostril or mouth activity might mean. However, there are exceptions to every rule. For example, Appaloosa horses sport breed-specific physical characteristics that range from their spotted coat and thin manes to naturally visible eye whites. An Appaloosa may appear shocked, judging from the appearance of their eyes, but they might actually be feeling 100% nonchalant. Some types of Arabian horses have larger than average nostrils; this trait serves well when performing in endurance-type sports, and has nothing to do with their overall attitude and sense of well-being.

As a result, it's a great idea to learn how to familiarize yourself with the overall message of a horse's body language. Of course, the best way to do that—in my experience—is to learn the various positions and expressions of each part of the face to put together and decode your horse's attempt to communicate with you.

A horse's ears have an impressive range of motion, and they can move independently. Typically a horse's ears swivel forward and backward to hear everything that is going on around them. While the position of a horse's eyes provides it with an expansive range of vision, the ears pivot like little satellite dishes to pick up any and all nearby transmissions. So, if your horse is standing still, looking otherwise calm but you notice their ears are twisting around a bit, this doesn't necessarily mean anything is immediately wrong but that your horse might need to be reminded that they need to pay attention to you, first. This can usually be accomplished with a little "QUIT" command, a tap on the shoulder, light pop of the lead rope, or in Red's case, calmly saying, "My dude, hello" and waving. Whatever works for that particular horse.

If the ears swivel towards the rear, stay facing the rear, and start to lower closer and closer to the ground, your horse is likely expressing displeasure. Generally speaking, the flatness of the ears is directly indicative of how upset they are, but again, this can change from horse to horse. In many cases, ears that are turned backward but still upright are similar to a human glare or strong side-eye, while ears that are invisibly tucked against the horse's skull are what we might deem "about to go nuclear" in another human. Ears that are perked straight upwards may mean the horse is hyper-focused on a particular sound, which can be a problem if they decide the source of that sound is potentially dangerous.

Looking at a horse's eyes will also give you some indication of how relaxed or focused they are. A non-threatened horse will generally look around at their surroundings. They may or may not move their heads to get a closer look at something that's moving or to follow their ears to determine what made a particular sound. For the most part, a horse looking around, and observing their surroundings is a good thing. If your horse becomes hyperfocused on a single point of interest, raising their head to get a better look, you might need to remind them that they need to follow your lead, again with a light vocal or physical reminder to pay attention to you. On the other hand, if your horse's head shoots straight up, exposing its eye whites as its eyes bulge outward, that's a very common sign that they feel very threatened, and they're close to acting upon that threat.

Nostrils can be tricky, not only because of the difference in shape and size between different horses, but because some horses are what I call "naturally woofle-y." A "naturally woofle-y" horse is literally nosey– instead of checking out the smells that come to them, they're on the lookout for something untoward and their rapidly flapping nostrils make a soft "woof-woof-woof" sound. Horses have a keen sense of smell, and just as their ears work as radars, their noses are constantly scanning the scents that float by for signs of danger or deliciousness. Horses can detect both enemies and the presence of food through scent, so it's common for a horse to occasionally take in a few wide, deep breaths to analyze a smell. But, if your horse has their nostrils flared to maximum capacity, it's a very good sign that their fight, flight, or freeze instinct has engaged. They're not just reading the room at this point, but concentrating on a particular threat.

Mouth activity is usually more straightforward. If the horse is actively gnashing its teeth or trying to nip at something, that is nearly always a sign that they are experiencing discomfort or anger. I personally cannot recall a case in which a horse chomped its teeth continuously or in the direction of a particular stimulating object in glee, but I don't want to exclude any particularly expressive horses, so I won't say "always." You may find your horse chomps repeatedly when you're tightening the girth of your saddle. This could be a sign of discomfort or just a bad habit your horse has picked up along the way. If the behavior is new, you might want to have them evaluated for ulcers, as this is a common way horses communicate belly pain.

A horse may stand quietly and chew with their mouth closed. This is frequently a sign of pleasure or being fully relaxed. Despite what some jokesters may try to tell you, horses are not ruminants, so they are not chewing their cud. They're simply moving their jaws because they're comfortable with what's going on around them. Happy horses may yawn or stick their tongue out, as well.

Then there are the many expressive faces horses pull when you've found their favorite scritchy-scratch spot. Horses can twitch their skin to rid themselves of bugs, roll in dirt, sand, or mud for that deep, full-body itch relief, and shake their entire body like dogs to flick debris from their body. They use their lips, teeth, and sometimes their hind legs to take care of tickly spots.

But there are some places they can't reach, and when you find those spots with your hands or curry comb, your horse will let you know by contorting its entire body to maximize the pleasure. They'll wiggle their lips from side to side, or smack them together while nodding their heads. They may put their upper lip straight up in the air like they're smiling. Known as Flehemen Face, this expression actually increases their ability to smell and can be associated with a very enjoyable grooming session, accidentally eating something they did not enjoy, or acknowledgment that a nearby mare is in estrus. My best advice in moments like these is to pull out your camera and take a few photos of your horse being goofy and happy because these are the moments you'll cherish forever.

In time, you may find yourself almost subconsciously tuned in to your horse's facial expressions. As a child, I was always fascinated by the seasoned horse people who could tell their horse to "knock it off" without looking up from grooming or tacking up. It is possible to become so tuned in to your horse's body language that you don't necessarily need to stop what you're doing to fully assess the complete message. Much as humans can learn other human languages with time, practice, and exposure, you may be able to learn not only your horse's method of communication but vernacular and accent, as well.

That being said, learning new languages is easier for some individuals, and harder for others. You are not a bad horse person for not picking up what they're putting down. It can take years of daily interaction with horses to really get a feel for what they're telling us, and some horses are more stoic while others are drama queens in their communication styles. You may need a translator– in the form of a trusted friend, trainer, or vet– to help you really appreciate your horse's vocabulary.

I've included a selection of corresponding articles and videos in the Resources section to provide a visual example of some of the things I've mentioned here. This can help you understand your horse's facial expressions better, and over time, you'll likely appreciate your horse's personality, opinions, and triggers enough to appreciate even more subtle expressions and commentary.

Chapter 2: Body Language

Technically speaking, facial expressions are part of the overall concept of body language, but I wanted to address what a horse's face is doing and what its body is doing separately because there can often be a disparity between the two.

As prey animals, a horse's first reaction to warning signals going off in their brain is to stand stock still and analyze the situation, generally through their senses of hearing, sight, and smell. Hence the pricked ears, wide eyes, and flared nostrils. Unless you look at the horse's face, you may not be aware that they are paying attention to something besides you.

That being said, there are some subtle differences between a horse standing stock still because they have no desire to move otherwise, and a horse who is working out whether or not it's time to bolt. The main difference is usually the amount of tension in your horse's body. A relaxed horse might be standing with its neck in a comfortable, natural position. They might have a hind leg relaxed, standing with one toe cocked and resting their weight on their other three legs.

A horse who is working out the probability of danger will likely have its head raised with its neck tall and vertical. They'll stand very upright, shifting their weight to both rear legs so they can launch in the appropriate direction to get away from impending doom.

A horse's body positioning can also tell you if they're experiencing discomfort, physically or mentally. Horses are instinctually programmed to move away from pressure, which we'll discuss a bit more in the section about training methods. If your horse is swinging their front or hind end away from you, that may be their way of telling you that something's wrong, and it would be great if you could investigate the situation further.

The word "discomfort" can mean a lot of different things, though. For example, a horse that has a sore hoof due to access or bruise may attempt to move the offending body part as far away from you as possible. They'll often shift their weight away from the sore side, or wave that leg in the air in an attempt to relieve the tremendous pressure and pain within their hoof. A horse who is back sore, experiencing skin irritations like rubs or fungus, or having a stomach ulcer flare-up, may scoot away from the pressure of the brush when you're grooming them. A horse who doesn't want its face or ears touched will do their best to remove them from your reach.

Your horse also has a singular communication device that we often forget: the tail. When we think about tail language, we typically think of a dog wagging its tail, or a cat puffing up their tail in alarm. Similarly, horses can be very expressive with their tails when the moment calls for it.

A horse's tail consists of the dock, which is part of the spine, and the skirt, which is the flesh and hair that comprise the exterior of a horse's tail. Tails can be very different from horse to horse, with some breeds having more vertebrae than others. Appaloosas tend to grow sparse, short tails, while Friesians and Gypsy Vanners have an unmerciful amount of tails (according to their groomers).

Muscles connecting along the horse's spine extend through the tail so that the horse can move it at will. Typically, a horse will swish their tail to ward off flies and other bothersome pests. They may use their tails as fans to circulate air around themselves on a sweltering day. Part protection and part air conditioning, a horse's swishing tail may mean nothing more than "it's a bit hot and buggy out here."

However, a tail can be used to communicate very exciting information. An angry horse will swish their tail aggressively. This differs from normal swishing due to the frequency and ferocity of the action. An extremely excited horse may raise their tail upwards and move rapidly with extended strides to demonstrate its pleasure, confusion, or fury.

Horses can also learn that humans find tail swishing threatening. I have known an experienced lesson horse or two who has tried to play the "I'm intimidating!" act when they simply want to continue hanging out in their stall or pasture.

Speaking of, when you enter your horse's stall, pasture, or enclosure, how do they respond? Do they turn their backsides to you and act like you aren't there? If you have cats at home, you may be familiar with this body positioning. It's a common expression of "I am displeased, and your presence is not alleviating this displeasure" in the animal kingdom. Horses generally exhibit this type of behavior when they're attempting to avoid leaving their current situation, frequently because they don't want to go to work. This may be due to pain or discomfort, or a bad habit they've picked up through their life experiences, so it's important to observe all of your horse's overall behavior to determine if this is normal for them, or a sign of possible trouble.

Now let's consider what happens when you interact or work with your horse. Does your horse pay attention to quite literally everything around themselves instead of you? When you mount up, does your horse scoot away from the mounting block quickly, or relax and let you get adjusted? A horse who is easily distracted can be dangerous since they're clearly not paying attention to the person in charge (you). The entire purpose of training is to encourage a horse to trust and communicate with you, so when they're scanning their surroundings and come across something to react to, they're not in a position of trust or communication– they're preoccupied and absent-minded. It's more or less the equine equivalent of holding onto a lit fuse, but not knowing what it's connected to, hoping that the thing that goes pop at the end will be manageable.

Your horse may be exceptionally distracted in a new environment, or when new horses enter its presence. That's a temporary reaction to understandably over-stimulating situations. But if your horse is regularly mistaken for a yearling stud due to its behavior, prancing, dancing, and wildly googly-eyeing everything daily, it is time to take some important next steps in training.

Chapter 3: Movement

There is a fine line between body language and movement, but for this discussion, body movement refers to specific gestures and actions a horse may perform when they're being obstinate, naughty, or particularly communicative.

Many horses give warning signals before they enter attack mode. For example, a horse who is thinking of kicking out with its hind legs, or bucking to bring its hindquarters fully in the air may hunch their rear end, pick up its hind legs rapidly, and even wag a raised leg in the air to mimic the action of a kick. Generally speaking, these actions are accompanied by backward ears to say, "Hey friend, I'm tolerating this, but not for much longer. Something needs to change."

A horse who is about to leave the premises in a hurry may prance in place or side to side as they figure out the best way to exit the situation. Horses may also wiggle side to side when they're trying to get away from an uncomfortable situation, such as a farrier asking them to pick up a sore leg, or a vet trying to administer a shot.

Backing quickly is another fun equine expression of disdain. And of course, by "fun," I mean "annoying and potentially dangerous." Horses are very capable of moving in reverse, barring certain spinal or lameness situations, and when they feel threatened, they can pull some *Smokey and Bandit*-level maneuvers. While they can't move backward quite as quickly as they can forward, it's still fast and powerful enough to snap a breakaway halter or light crossties or cause serious damage to the muscles, tendons, and bones in your arms, shoulder, and back.

In most cases, the direction your horse wants to move will indicate the source of their terror or discomfort. As mentioned, horses move away from pressure, real or perceived. Sometimes, normally well-behaved horses can get a bit squiggly when they're trying to avoid something unpleasant. Ideally, your horse will give you plenty of clues about their emotions, especially when you combine their facial expressions, body language, and movement into a complete message.

By observing both the scene around you and your horse's attempts at communication, you can generally piece together what is triggering this response, and what's about to happen. This may take time, and while often it is obvious after the fact that Patch nipping at Henry, while Henry was spooking at Hillary pushing the wheelbarrow, caused Jennifer to scream, which in turn spooked Henry, which then caused your horse to rear and snap the cross ties, these multiple steps to doom may not lead to an immediate conclusion in the heat of the moment. As you watch your horse slide and stumble as it attempts to gain purchase to launch into a gallop on a concrete aisleway, you are not going to be thinking, "Hmm... I wonder how this happened, and whether my horse provided obvious body language that I missed."

Instead, it's going to be a long process of watching and noticing subtle differences in your horse's behavior when they're relaxed, feeling good, uncomfortable, or in a rotten mood. Watching multiple body parts and movements simultaneously may feel complicated at first, but you'll likely start to recognize patterns pretty quickly. If your horse whips their head to the left to nip at you as you're tightening the girth every single time you tighten the girth, but no other time, the cause of the reaction is very clear.

On the other hand, a horse who doesn't want to do something may exhibit similar body language cues to explain a simple message of, "I don't want to; you can't make me." So how do you determine if your horse is triggered by a significant stimulus and needs to be desensitized to a situation, or if they're being ornery and need to be trained to give up the attitude?

That's where the rest of the body language package comes in. Your horse's facial expression can tell you a lot about how they're actually feeling. Are their teeth bared in anger or frustration, or are their eyes practically rolling in their heads because they've lost control of their physical reactions due to fear? Are they actively attempting to get away from something that has frightened them, or are they stoically refusing to do what is being asked?

A horse who is afraid will generally act on pure instinct, while a horse who is being stubborn will often act deliberately evasive– that is until they are provoked into feeling threatened, at which point pure instinct will take over. For this reason, horse training can be challenging. Knowing that there's a grey area between thoughtful and instinctive reactions, and understanding exactly where and how generous or tiny your horse's grey area is, can be one of the most important things to grasp when working with an ill-behaved horse.

When we're confronted with our horse's bad behavior, we often feel pressured to do something about it right then. But that's not how horses work. Yes, it's important to take care of the current situation immediately, clean up any messes, and make amends as necessary. But the process of observing, understanding, and finding the right course of action for changing the offending behavior isn't going to happen overnight. Instead, it's going to be a process, and it might just take a village, as the saying goes.

Chapter Four

Evaluating the Stages of Naughtiness

S o far, I've referred to your horse's behavior in relation to your comfort level in somewhat vague terms. "If you think you can handle it," "You can call in a trainer," "If you don't feel comfortable," etc. Now we need to differentiate between the stages, levels, and potential escalation of your horse's behavior to determine where this behavior lies.

To do this, we need to have a full picture of what's happening, why it's happening, how your horse reacts, how you react, and how much warning you get before the naughtiness occurs. In each preceding section, we've discussed what to look for, how to look for it, and potential interpretations. This is how we determine how serious things are, and what our next steps may include. This is why I urged you not to sell your horse and move into a cave–this is the fun part!

You may be thinking that "fun" is the last word you'd use to describe your horse's behavior, and you might be concerned about my mental health for even associating "fun" with what is currently happening. Please note that I'm not making light of any dangerous situation—it's just that this is the point where you truly become a horse person, deciphering a strongly worded and heavily coded message from a four-legged fuzzy beast into behavior that makes sense and can be redirected. This is the moment the sleuth solves the case; the mystery is solved, and now everyone can proceed with the truth out in the open

Therefore, we need to pull together all of our observations thus far:

- Step 1: What behavioral problems does your horse have? How is your horse in their stall? Can you and other people handle your horse without fearing for your lives? Are you aware of any particular triggers or scenarios that set your horse off?

- Step 2: What is your horse doing? Are they bolting, kicking, rearing, spooking, biting, becoming uncatchable, or freestyling their own particular brand of misbehavior?

- Step 3: What are you doing and what have you already done? From your own instinctive reactions to actual attempts to provide redirection to your horse's behavior, reflect on what you do when your horse acts undesirably.

- Step 4: What are your horse's "tells?" What are they doing right before disaster strikes?

- Step 5: How urgently does this behavior need attention? How much time and effort are you able to invest in this situation?

The order of these steps is somewhat arbitrary because there might be a lot of watching, observing, reflecting, changing your mind, and watching again to see if you observe something different, or if you had it right the first time. The human memory is an unreliable narrator, especially when our brains are super-charged with emotions or adrenaline.

You may wish to keep a journal or chart of things that you observe to figure out what the pattern is. As I've said many times, the situation may be bigger or more complex than you have imagined, and it won't change if you're not working with your horse on the thing that's setting them off.

I once worked with a lovely Thoroughbred ex-racehorse who was consistently lovely, curious, affectionate, and obedient. His natural posture was head up, ears pricked, woofer-ing around to find interesting smells, but he kept his feet and teeth to himself. One day, as I was cleaning his feet, his head shot up further than I could've imagined, he yanked his hoof away from me, charged backward to the end of the cross ties, snapped the cross ties, turned himself around and bolted into our indoor arena, where he galloped himself in circles before stopping and walking over to me as nothing had happened.

I assumed–foolishly, of course–that he had been spooked by something I couldn't see when I was bent over, and we spent the rest of our work session sorting out hoof picking and cross ties so I could attempt to recreate the source of his panic. Other than being a little wary and snorty about ending up in the cross-ties again, there was no encore performance.

I even further foolishly assumed that the issue was closed and done when it didn't happen again...at least until it did happen again.

I will skip the long and arduous process of figuring it out because it took several months and experimentation to discover that the horse had allergies, and the combination of mucus drainage and almost invisible hives in the thick hair around his ears that were being irritated by the halter when he threw his head up, caused him to freak out. Horses regularly spook at the noise made when they break the wind, so this is not entirely out of character for the species. It just wasn't the first thing anyone would have considered for a potential training issue.

The horse in question was brought back to physical health with a series of allergy shots and antibiotics to treat a mild sinus infection, and afterward, retraining him to stand politely in the crossties was a little bit of a process. Since we'd been looking in the wrong direction, he had worked up a bit of a trauma response to being tied. He expected serious pain and itchiness on his head and ears, and he expected that there would be yelling and consequences when he bolted because his fuzzy little brain and body couldn't handle the discomfort any longer. As a result, he was nervous in the cross-ties for a long time. Still, we spoke to him kindly, reassured him, stayed calm around him, and let him sniff out the situation until he was satisfied it would be all right in the end.

Once you've figured out what's going on, you can gauge what the ideal next steps for you and your horse may be. Let's walk through the stages of naughtiness to get a feel for where you are now, and what you might need to do to enact change.

Chapter 1: Things You Can Improve Alone

Before we get started, I'd like to remind you that no horse person should feel that they have no choice but to "deal with it alone." There can be a million reasons why you might not consider it feasible to work with your horse's behavior problems on your own, including:

- Your age/the horse's age

- Your health/the horse's health

- Outlying conditions, like being pregnant, coming back from an injury/surgery, etc–again, considering both you and the horse

- Your experience with horses

- Your own sense of fear and danger

There's an old saying in the equine community: "Green plus green equals black and blue." The meaning behind this saying is that pairing an inexperienced horse with an inexperienced handler frequently results in injury. While I've mentioned several times throughout my books that bumps and bruises are borderline inevitable, we equestrians don't actively seek injury or threat to our personal health. The choices you make and the boundaries you set may be based on the factors I've listed above or not– know that the choices you make are valid as long as they honor the safety and well-being of you, your horse, and any bystanders.

However, there are some instances wherein you might need to at least reinforce behaviors alone. For example, if your horse is a stall kicker, it is unreasonable to think that a trainer or behaviorist will come to your barn every time your horse starts beating on the walls. Instead, there may be times that you have to enact whatever communication and correction methods your professional has assigned to you.

That, however, is different from coming up with your own plan for resolution and acting on it. I've said that working with horses is often a curious thing, in that you may think you're going to work on this or accomplish that today, but your horse will alert you that you have another thing coming. This is true under saddle, in hand, and when working on attitude issues.

A horse who doesn't want to do something–anything!- will often go out of their way to make sure they don't have to. So, once your horse has made up their mind that they are going to react to a certain scenario or trigger, it will avoid having to learn any other options. Just as you might take a stubborn toddler by the hand and walk them into the grocery store while they're having a meltdown, you might need to consistently keep your horse's attention focused and feet moving forward (or not moving at all, depending on the situation). That can be difficult.

Assess how comfortable you are leading your horse. How well do you think you can gain and hold your horse's attention? How comfortable do you feel with tools like stud chains and lunge whips? Do you have enough control of your emotions that you can repeat the same two steps forward and a hundred steps back for hours, days, or months?

Once I pulled Red from the field where he was slowly being starved and took him to my friend's barn, he decided he was "Home." As in, he would not leave the property. In many cases, once a horse is "Home," they quite rightly don't venture out. But I had plans to the contrary. I wanted to take him on trail rides at the local nature preserves, and I wanted to drive him over to a nearby barn that had a warm indoor arena in the winter. Additionally, it's a good idea to have a horse that's willing to hop on a trailer in case of a medical emergency!

But, Red wasn't having it. Each time I attempted to load him onto a trailer, he would plant his feet and refuse to move. Occasionally, he would start backing up rapidly, but only until he got away from the person tugging at his face. He wasn't being particularly dangerous, but it was super irritating to pay a $30 arena fee and only get to enjoy 10 minutes of riding time because your horse won't leave his home.

It took months of work, and when I say "two steps forward; ten back," I actually mean that literally. Each session, we would creep towards the trailer, sniff the ramp or step up, put a few feet on the trailer, then rapidly back up about 20-30 feet. Then I'd have to, again, coax him towards the trailer, where he would sniff the ramp, and rapidly back up about 20-30 feet.

Now, there are loads of different methods for helping a hard loader realize that the trailer is not to be feared. One involves using a lunge whip on the ground behind the horse to gently urge the horse to move forward. Red, who likes to pick up whips in his own mouth and bang on things that make loud noises in his spare time, decided that a lunge whip was extraordinarily insulting in this situation, so when I tried that method, he reared up and almost landed on my car. That is the perfect example of doing something that should work, but unintentionally escalating the situation.

If you are not willing, able, or excited about having to work on the same scenario/trigger for extended periods of time, with the possibility that you might try something that makes things worse, it is completely rational to call a professional. While adjusting your horse's behavior is the ultimate goal, that goal is not going to be met unless everyone, including the horse, is feeling generally safe and confident.

It turns out, the best way to get Red on a trailer is to pat him, coax him, and have a little grain waiting at the front. He likes to put his front feet in the trailer first to feel how his balance is going to change, and then he feels confident hopping in. Unless he's going Home, in which case all I have to say is, "We're Going Home, Buddy!" and he leaps in the trailer gleefully. Horses are capable of understanding far more than we realize.

If your horse is doing something pretty straightforward, like rushing past you when you turn them out or spooking at the flag at the end of the arena, this may be something you can get through with frequently repeated correction. You might need to incorporate some new tools like a thick pair of leather gloves and a heavy lead rope to stop the rushing. You may also need to try new methods, like lunging your horse day after day in a part of the arena that triggers their flight instincts. Like the Thoroughbred I mentioned earlier, you may find yourself trying everything you can think of.

I strongly recommend to anyone who is experiencing ongoing issues with their horse do all the research they can to figure it out. That may mean typing your horse's exact behavior into a search engine. That may mean reading every book you can on the subject (and thank you for choosing mine as one of your options!). You may obsessively watch videos of professionals working with similarly-minded horses to see what you might be able to use for your own horse. You may also head to the Resources section at the end of this book to help you get started.

My personal recommendation is to do what you can, as you can, and if that doesn't stop the behavior or build communication and trust between you and your horse, then it's a good idea to call a professional. In the meantime, however, keep observing your horse. The more you learn about this peculiar behavior, the more clues you have about the causes and mitigating factors.

Today's smartphones are a fantastic tool for horse folks because we can finally use a pocket-sized device to take a detailed video of our horses that we can then play back, share with others, and use to catalog different events. Take pictures or videos of your horse misbehaving to see if you can gain even more clues about its triggers and responses.

Yes, a professional should be able to help you diagnose the situation and come up with meaningful ways you and your horse can work through it together, but you see and interact with your horse far more than any other individual. Use this connection—or lack thereof, depending on the behavior—to help guide your methods of behavior adjustment.

And in case I haven't fully made my point about safety, please consider wearing gloves, a helmet, and a body protector, and having a helper nearby who can at least dial the phone for an ambulance if necessary. Always put safety first—a rude horse can wait, but even run-of-the-mill injuries can be frustrating for a lifetime.

Chapter 2: When to Call a Professional

Once you've decided you need professional assistance, you need to decide who you're going to call.

As I mentioned in *Why Does My Horse Act Like This: Understanding Equine Behavior in Your New Horse,* the frequent cause for misbehavior is pain or physical discomfort. So, the first professional you may wish to call could be a veterinarian, farrier, chiropractor, or equine dentist. If I had followed my own advice here, I wouldn't have spent weeks trying to get that poor former racehorse to behave in the crossties when he was trying to tell me that he had open sores on the backs of his ears.

Once your horse is examined, it will either receive a clean bill of health, or the professional will provide you with instructions on how to help your horse become more comfortable. I have seen corrective shoeing and good dental float work miracles on some cranky horses, so this is always a reasonable path to explore. If you have limited funds for equine interventions, as many of us do, I strongly recommend putting them towards your horse's health and wellness before you start the search for a trainer.

You may also wish to contact a saddle fitter if you notice your horse is acting up only when you ride. In today's society, many of us joke that horses are doing us a favor by allowing us to ride them, so make sure you've got a bit and bridle that fit your horse's mouth and face and a saddle that fits their back. A saddle fitter can look at the equipment you've been using to ensure it's not the source of discomfort and help you make adjustments if it is.

You may wish to contact a horse behaviorist for advice. These individuals work almost entirely on the ground and use their finely-tuned ability to read equine body language to get a feel for what they're doing and why. Then, they typically work with the horse for a while to understand what types of reactions they have, when they have them, why they have them, and what works best to get their attention and keep it. Most equine behavior experts will work with your horse to create pressure, gauge how they work with you, and communicate their needs. As a result, you'll have professional insight into your horse's behavior, as well as tips and tools for increasing your equine communication skills.

A trainer's role is typically very similar in that they will work with your horse and evaluate its behavior. However, while a behavior specialist's goal is to open up communication to avoid evasive behavior, a trainer will generally put a stop to the horse's bad manners and teach them how to "act right."

You may hear of some equine professionals referred to as "cowboys." While this frequently refers to actual professionals who work with cattle, horses, and livestock, there may be times when you hear the term out of that context. Generally speaking, these cowboys are folks who aren't full-time trainers, but they volunteer to do the dirty work when it comes to breaking out a horse. They've earned their title due to being able to jump on, stay on, and safely eject themselves from very green horses who do not warm up to the idea of saddle training. Trainers often hire cowboys to work with them to help them with the really dangerous stuff. Occasionally, cowboys will hang out their shingles as a trainer and accept some projects that they feel will help them build their credentials. Though the term is often associated with the type of trainer who will use "quick fixes" and potentially harsh treatment, that's not always the case. Anyone who works with your horse should be vetted for suitability, regardless of their job title.

When horses are put in training, it's typically for months at a time. Trainers will frequently put 30, 60, or 90 days of training on a particular beast. The length of time a horse spends with a trainer usually depends on how much the horse's owner wants said beast to learn, and how willing the horse is to learn. Your horse may stay at the trainer's facility for this period—which means you'll have to pay board—or your trainer may elect to come to your horse's location a certain number of times each week.

Trainers rarely work on just one issue, unless it's a thoroughly compounded and deep-rooted issue. Horses who have been deeply traumatized, for example, will typically have a few different triggers to deal with, which can pop up in a variety of situations. You may not even be aware of how sincere your horse is about their feelings on a particular matter because once that instinct kicks in, things escalate quickly. Therefore, a trainer will work towards a particular goal, and help kick any other triggers, habits, or aggressions that might be stirred up throughout the process.

Trainers can also help us, the horse's person, work through any triggers, habits, or aggressiveness that we might display, as well. Since your horse is constantly gauging your body language and communication as well, you may be accidentally telling your horse that everything is terrible and they need to be on high alert. Knowing how to act, what to do, and how to respond to your horse's flights of fancy can help you feel more confident in working with your horse daily.

Finding a trainer can be an involved process, however. In *Why Does My Horse Act Like This: Understanding Equine Behavior in Your New Horse,* we discussed the qualities to look for in a trainer. Again, I don't want to be too repetitive, but I strongly recommend:

- Meeting the trainer in person

- Touring their facility and meeting their personal horses

- Bringing them to where your horse lives to get a feel for their daily life and routine

- Watching them work

- Asking for references and following up to get these individuals' take on the trainer's abilities

- Asking trusted professionals in your area what they think of this trainer

- Sharing the information you've received from your vet, farrier, chiropractor, etc. when coming up with a training plan

You may also ask if you can be present when the trainer works with your horse, as possible given your schedule. I personally find it very suspicious if a trainer says I cannot be there, though there are some scenarios wherein it's a good idea for the trainer to work with a horse alone. For example, your trainer may want to see if your horse's behavior is replicated when you aren't around. On the whole, though, your trainer should encourage you to participate in your horse's growth and development so that you can help your horse maintain their good manners.

Another neat thing most people don't realize is that you can pull your horse from training. Depending on the contract you sign (and you should always sign a contract detailing expectations, time frames, and expenses), you may forfeit your payment by doing this. However, if you feel your horse is not responding to your trainer's methodology, or you feel uncomfortable with the process, you may wish to pursue this opportunity.

Ultimately, the intervention of a professional should help you feel more confident and understanding of your horse's particular issues. While the opinion of equine professionals will rarely cause your horse's behavior to change immediately, the goal of all professionals should be to work with you and your horse within your means and ability to help find harmony. That will likely mean change and compromise for you and your horse, but that's really what building a relationship with a horse is. Learning how to work with each other and communicate effectively is really the best part of sharing our lives with our equine companions. At least, that's my take on it!

Chapter 3: When to Give Up – and How

There seems to be this general idea that once you choose to share your life with a horse, there's no getting out of it. Indeed, many of us become strongly bonded to our horses and choose to move heaven and Earth to ensure that we're able to live together for as long as possible. Most behavioral issues are a mere hiccup or blip in the overall relationship, and once communication has been established and attitudes adjusted all around, that wonderful relationship resumes.

But just because that's the norm doesn't mean it ends up that way every time. You may find that your horse's behavioral issues are more than you can handle. You may become very frightened of your horse, which can escalate the situation until it spirals far out of your control. You may wonder why you're spending half of your paycheck on an animal you can't stand to be around. You may have been injured or traumatized by your horse's actions, and are physically unable to take matters into your own hands. Trainers can be expensive, and you may not be able to swing the extra cost. Or, the stark reality may dawn on you that you and this creature are simply not meant to be friends.

Many people feel that adopting an animal of any species and bringing them into your home means you're signing on to care for them until the very end. That is true, but while some people define "the end" as "the end of life" for either pet or person, my years in equine rescue and training have taught me that it's best to consider it "the end of the partnership."

It could very well be that you and your horse are simply ill-suited for each other. Whether you have a personality clash, or they aren't comfortable in the living situation you can provide for them, it is ok to admit that this is simply not the horse for you. It is **not** ok to pretend like nothing is happening and wait for the problem to go away on its own.

When I worked at a rescue facility, we would frequently have our stalls filled with emaciated horses with skin sores and overgrown hooves at the end of the year. When the sun came out and the weather turned nice, well-intentioned folks would decide to follow their dreams of owning a horse. But once the horse began to act in a way the new owners couldn't handle, these folks became frightened of the horse. Instead of doing anything about it right away, they would neglect the horse. They were too terrified to bring them in from the field or go into their stalls to feed them or interact with them in any way.

Horses have a strong survival instinct, so they tend to find ways to survive. But the less you communicate with your horse, the less the horse will return the favor. Instead of leaning on their established knowledge, they'll revert to feral horse ways, working on staying alive over greeting humans with a friendly nicker and being polite.

As a result, these well-meaning people would be embarrassed at their perceived failure, ignore the horses until the guilt was too great, and then have no idea what to do with them. Since the horses were lame and unhealthy due to lack of care, they would bring them to the rescue. You see, all of those big fancy barns with gleaming horses and loving, caring humans aren't in the market for skinny horses who will need thousands of dollars in vet and farrier work to be sound and happy again. Once your neglect—however well-meaning you thought you were–has impacted your horse's health, the number of safe, kind, happy homes you can find for that horse has dropped sharply.

Therefore, I strongly encourage everyone to take care of their horses (and all other animals) with the absolute best standard of care until the end of your relationship. If you find that you cannot establish the right relationship with your horse, start looking for a new home immediately. The longer you wait to find your horse a home, the lesser chance you have of that being a fantastic home where your horse will thrive.

Here's my recommended approach for this process:

Step 1: Contact the former owner if possible. Explain what the horse is doing, and ask kindly if that's a new behavior or something they've observed in the past. You may be surprised at how much information wasn't mentioned at the time of purchase. Imagine my shock when I described what Belle was doing to her former owner, and she replied, "Oh, haven't you been giving her an ulcer supplement?"

I also recommend having the difficult "what if this doesn't work out?" conversation during the purchase process. Not all folks are willing or able to take back a horse they've sold, but they may also have resources you can connect with to potentially rehome your horse. Each time I've sold a horse, I've included all of my contact information (email, and phone), as well as the name of a local rescue I trust. I do not guarantee that I can actively take the horse back, but I am willing to do my best to help them find a new home for the horse if they would like assistance.

All of this being said, it's important to remember that the horse's former owner sold them for a reason–because they were no longer willing or able to care for them. Once you have paid for the horse and signed the bill of sale (always get a bill of sale), the former owner rarely has any legal obligations towards you and the horse. Therefore it is possible that this path may not be lucrative, or even available to you. That's when we move to Step 2.

Step 2: At this point, you might consider contacting local trainers, cowboys, and lesson barns to see if they require a project horse. Be transparent about why you are not keeping the horse.

A "project horse" needs some work before they're fully considered an Equine Good Citizen. They may be very green, have some bad habits, or just need to get back into consistent work after an extended time off due to illness, injury, or any other reason. A project horse who does not need to be completely rehabilitated is a diamond in the rough, and many trainers, cowboys, or lesson barns with a bevy of experienced amateurs looking to bring up their own horse will jump on the opportunity to obtain a healthy horse, even if it does come with a few "idiosyncrasies."

If your horse is a decent being when at work, you might contact a local chapter of 4H or the United States Pony Club to see if they have any members who might be a good fit for your horse. I actually managed to rehome a horse who was not a good fit for me through Pony Club members networking across the country to find the perfect family for him.

You may also wish to speak with your vet, farrier, chiropractor, feed supplier, and other equine or farm-related professionals in your area. They may also know someone looking for a horse just like yours.

Years ago, I was leasing Red to a friend who lived on the other side of the state. When the lease was coming to an end, I was struggling to find a place to put him for the time being. Amazingly enough, a very nice lady who ran an equine therapy facility stopped in to grab a bottle from the winery where I worked. She was the only customer, so we started talking. A few weeks later, she was Red's new lessee, and she loved having him around until her lease ended. Reach out to anyone you can think of who might know someone who knows someone!

Step 3: Post sales information everywhere you can online. Some social media platforms allow for horse sales groups and sales ads, but not all of them, so check the rules to avoid getting yourself banned.

There are many online sales websites for horses, and I've linked a few in the Resources section. Proceed with caution because it's very easy to find and fall in love with a horse via these sites– that's how I found Red! Some may offer free options for advertising a horse for sale, while others involve a fee or commission. Check the details before you get started.

Step 4: If you are getting to the point where you don't think anyone will take your horse, it's time to call a rescue. Explain that you are surrendering your horse, and be honest about the problems you've had. The first rescue may not be able to take your horse, but they should be able to help you find additional resources to reach out to. You may also be invited to check out the rescue facility to get a feel for the care they will provide for your horse. Many rescues in the United States are private 501(c)(3) organizations, which means they're funded by donations and run by volunteers. As a result, some rescues are gorgeous and immaculate, while others are fueled by a bunch of horse-crazy volunteers shoveling manure and administering medication between conference calls, Zoom meetings, and school obligations.

Another common question I get is "How do you make sure you get your money back when you sell a horse." You do not. There is rarely a positive return on investment or ROI on a horse. Grand Prix and Masters level performance horses, racehorses, and horses who break into the show business are some of the only horses I know who have come close to recouping their overall cost. Horses cost a lot–mentally, physically, emotionally, and monetarily.

Furthermore, the horse market changes a lot. In 2008, horses became very inexpensive, thanks to the financial events of the year and the drop in equine sports participation. I worked at the rescue then, and our stalls were packed with horses who were relatively healthy and needed a minor tune-up to be productive beasts. Their owners had simply lost their jobs and couldn't afford them any longer. The average monthly cost per horse at that particular facility, at that specific point in time, was about $275. We were adopting the horses out at $100 each. No ROI here!

So, if you are frustrated by someone "low-balling" you on the purchase of your horse, you will need to consider which is more important to you: the money, or knowing your horse is likely going to a decent home. Either option is valid–I cannot judge someone for wanting the money they need to keep a roof over their head and meals in their bellies–but remember, a horse who is not being fed, cared for and trained properly will be harder to rehome. The faster your horse is sold or placed, the more immediate the financial impact of the sale, too.

That being said, if a good home for your horse is important to you, feel empowered to ask questions of any potential buyer to get a feel for their standards of care and the type of home your horse will have going forward. Your horse is your responsibility until the bill of sale is signed and they are transported to their new home.

Whichever path you choose, know that your choice is valid, as are all the feelings you have about your decision. While I consider myself an experienced horse person, I have hired trainers to help me in areas where I lacked experience and learned a lot in the process. A good trainer can really help open up communication between a human and a horse, which can make an already good relationship phenomenal.

I have also had to rehome a horse, as I mentioned earlier. It was a very difficult decision, based on my life situation at the time. The main consideration was that I had injured my spine, and I couldn't work with him in the way that he needed to be worked with. I attempted to find a leasing home for him, but ultimately, he went to a family in another state who rode him daily, took weekly lessons with him, and went trail riding with him several times a week. It was perfect for him, and I love getting photo updates of his shenanigans.

It is entirely up to you how you choose to deal with your horse's behavioral issues. Please be aware that they will not resolve themselves. Your horse will still need to be fed, watered, and cared for. The more you handle your horse, the more opportunities you have to establish communication with them. In turn, that gives you a greater chance of working out the problematic behavior, if you choose to do so. Just be sure to keep everyone's safety in mind, and know that it is not shameful to look for help.

If you choose to look for help, take the time to get the right helper for you and your horse. Whether that's someone who can help you support your horse physically–like a vet–or a behaviorist or trainer, you're looking for someone who can help you and your horse. Your goal is to learn and grow as a horse person, while your professional's goal is to identify the source of the behavior and help the horse understand why it's inappropriate.

But sometimes, there are issues between a horse and its human that even the best trainers can't resolve. Have you ever met a person and thought you might become friends, only to discover after hanging out a few times that you didn't enjoy each other's presence that much? You can't train away that lack of chemistry. You also can't train away money issues or find a magic supplement to feed your horse that will quell your fears.

When you purchased your horse, you signed on to be responsible for its well-being until the end of your relationship. That relationship may change. Just make sure you choose the most responsible path for your horse and yourself.

Chapter Five

The Great Debates

A s you search for possible solutions to your horse's puzzling behavior, you will find that there are many different training and communication methods. You will also find that horse people either accept that there are many potential tools to add to the horse training toolbox, or they vehemently and exhaustively oppose or uphold specific methods. There are those who swear by Pat Parelli's horsemanship methods, those who view them as some sort of bizarre joke, and those who view some of his theories as helpful, but not necessarily all of them. I do not make judgments on a trainer's methods until I get a feel for their process. I also believe that no two horses will respond exactly the same to the same training methods. This is also true of humans—it's simply not reasonable to expect two people to learn and work identically. I believe that if we get locked into a method, program, or theory without exploring other possibilities, we're doing a great injustice to our horses and ourselves. We can't learn and grow unless we quite literally step out of our comfort zones to appreciate and understand new information.

That being said, there are some training methods and theories that I find more dangerous than effective. You'll find that most horse people have a pretty firm stance towards things they feel are abusive versus potentially beneficial. Similarly, some people have indelible opinions about rewarding horses. Ultimately, no training is cruel, dangerous, or abusive unless it is taken past the regard for the long-term well-being of the horse and human.

To illustrate this point, I'd like to discuss a couple of the most popular debates on equine training and building good manners. These are not black-and-white issues; in fact, there are many "if/then" or "yes, but" statements that can be issued in either debate. I'll present the facts with as little bias as possible to allow you to make your decisions.

Debate 1 - Quick Fixes: Efficient or Dangerous?

Horse people are known for their bizarre and genius uses for simple and common items, like duct tape and baling twine. We like quick fixes because we like it when things are immediately taken care of at the least possible expense. That allows us to move more quickly onto the next disaster. There is no lack of disasters for horse people. Whether the fence is coming down, the insulation is being chewed up by the birds, or raccoons have figured out how to get in the feed room again, something always needs our attention. Throw in our natural human appreciation for immediate gratification, and the "quick and easy" way may seem very tempting.

Often in the horse world, "quick and easy" involves tools that teach horses not to do a certain thing by providing pain or pressure when they do that exact thing. Hobbles are used to bind a horse's rear legs together so that if they feel inclined to buck or kick, they'll be unable to land on their feet. Draw reins put pressure on a horse's mouth when they raise its head, encouraging them to release their necks downwards. Side reins have a similar purpose, but are used when a horse is not being ridden, which means they're fighting the pressure they're inflicting on themselves. Certain bits create discomfort on the bars of a horse's mouth or tongue to prevent them from ignoring their rider's hands. Stud chains create pressure across a horse's nose and face to make raising their heads uncomfortable.

Other tools are used to create performance. Some gaited horses wear padding and chains that encourage them to exaggerate their natural gaits. Certain breeds of horses with a naturally high-set tail will be shown with skin irritants applied to the underside of the dock to cause the horse to hold their tails even higher. Spurs and crops are used as an extension of a rider's leg to request more hind leg action from a horse under saddle.

Most of these tools are not harmful in theory but can be in practice. A horse left in their stall on hobbles can damage themselves if they land in a strange position or get stuck by a wall with no way to get up. Draw reins, side reins, and training bits in harsh and impatient hands can damage a horse's neck and mouth as they fight the pressure. Horses have been known to react dramatically to this type of pressure by rearing and flipping backward to escape. These actions can be fatal to both horses and humans. Light padding can be beneficial and even therapeutic, but heavy padding can impact the shape and movement of a horse's muscles, tendons, and ligaments over time. Using spurs and crops too much can tell a horse that they don't need to respond to more subtle commands, while possibly causing skin injury if used injudiciously.

Additionally, we have to take into consideration whether we really want to cause our horses pain. Momentary discomfort and pressure are one thing, but extended periods of being asked to do something that is beyond the horse's natural capability are different. Most horses respond to pressure instantly. However, that response may be to stop, look at you, and listen to what you are trying to communicate, or it may be to react even more defensively. Worst of all, you don't know what reaction a horse may have until you try, which can potentially mean you have one shot to either train or traumatize the horse with these tools.

There are horse people who believe in, and are physically and mentally capable of continuing, the escalation process with a horse until the horse gives up. Some trainers are willing to trip and flip horses to assert dominance, or who will wrestle horses to the ground to demonstrate why they want to consider this human their leader. Some trainers believe that encouraging a horse to fear them is a good way to prevent aggressive behavior from the horse. The theory behind these training processes is the natural pecking order found in horse herds. Horses physically duke it out to assert dominance over their herd members both in the wild and the pasture. If a human exerts physical dominance over a horse, then clearly that horse will think of that human as the head of the herd. The faster this is done, the more quickly the trainer can move forward with the horse's progress.

The trainers who employ quick fixes, like harsh or exaggerated use of tools, or using fear and pain as motivators argue that these methods are not only faster since they drive home the point immediately, but more effective in the long run because the horse learns to not argue with the human from the onset. This means that more meaningful training is more immediate. For example, if a horse is intended to hit the show circuit in time for the Nationals, they need to knock off the attitude and nasty behavior immediately so it can focus on the skills necessary to help them succeed in the show circuit. In other cases, a trainer will intentionally attempt to "break a horse's spirit" so that they can be safe in any situation, with any rider, and hopefully never act out.

Others feel that this method of exerting dominance over a horse is too much, too quickly. Following the "Ask, Tell, Demand" principles of horsemanship, a trainer should escalate from the lightest request for an action to the harshest insistence over some time, allowing the horse to process and respond to the request. Horses can pick up and react to even the most minute changes in body language, so why stress them out with physical and mental pain when a simple change in how you stand with the horse can accomplish the same result over time and with repetition?

Like the great debate over spanking children in the human world, there are a lot of "yes, but" statements between both sides. For example, some people believe that hitting a horse harshly with a whip as a form of defense (such as if a horse is charging towards you) is acceptable, as long as it is not used consistently. There are many arguments for how any training method can be cruel if done improperly, and any training method could also be considered a safety measure if used appropriately.

At the same time, many people agree that there is no such thing as "common" usage of tools and quick-fix training techniques, too. That is, there are ways to use these tools and techniques inadequately, effectively, or inhumanely. But remember that horses, like toddlers, all have different outlooks towards and tolerance for change, both of which can be unpredictable. What one horse tolerates well might be a terribly traumatic event to another horse. And, when you take into account that humans may act differently each day, depending on their mood, how they slept, what they've eaten, or how things are going so far that day, it is possible to be harsher with tools and techniques than consciously intended.

Quick fixes are generally effective, and the "quick" part is not often a misnomer. But the potential for injury is high, and some horses will fight against these methods literally, and sadly, to the death. Improperly used tools and techniques can result in spinal, skeletal, and structural damage that may be irreversible due to the fast and extreme way a horse's body may be conditioned. Other injuries, such as cuts and lacerations, will likely heal, though scarring is a concern, especially if you plan to take a horse into the show pen.

As a horse owner, it is up to you to determine how forceful you get with your horse's training. Whether that's using these tools and techniques yourself, or hiring a trainer who will use these methods on your horse, it is up to you to observe and decide how well your horse is tolerating them, and whether you are comfortable with the process and the results.

Debate 2 - To Treat or Not to Treat?

If you're wondering how treats could possibly be considered a bad thing, you're not alone. Everyone loves treats, right? That's actually the problem. Some horses really love treats–to the point where they'll become aggressive about them.

Horses have large teeth that are designed for grinding roughage all day. They can, do, and will use their mouth, lips, and teeth to communicate all sorts of messages, including pleasure and pain. Sometimes, that includes biting. While a horse lightly nipping at another horse is generally their way of saying, "Hey buddy–watch out!" that same light nip might cause a nasty bruise or open wound on our thin human skin. Therefore, we must teach our horses that they need to keep their mouths to themselves when humans are involved and choose another form of communication.

Yet, in the same breath, we also place a flat palm full of treats under a horse's nose and expect them to gingerly use their lips and tongue to retrieve them. Most horses have no problem with this, but some horses can get really nasty about this, aggressively snapping at humans whenever they want to be left alone, fed, or bored.

Some trainers feel that there is a direct correlation between hand-feeding treats and increased aggressive biting behavior. Some feel that the validity of this potential link really depends on the horse, their lifestyle, and any changes in their lives. Some feel that this is all a bunch of bunk and that treats are the best way to train a horse.

In a training scenario, a horse is typically offered a treat as an incentive for doing something "good," like walking towards the trainer, stretching its neck and back, or allowing the trainer to touch them in a ticklish or uncomfortable place. Occasionally, horses are offered treats as a distraction, just as you might offer a toddler a lollipop while they're getting a shot at the doctor's office.

The most common time a horse is offered treats is at the end of a work session. Many riders, drivers, and handlers praise their horses after a particularly enjoyable and educational practice with a handful of treats.

Anything your horse likes to eat can be considered a treat. Apples and carrots are some of the more well-known options, but there are many different types of equine yummies to choose from. Some feed companies will make treats that address a certain issue, providing probiotics for gastric support or joint supplements for reducing pain and inflammation. Some treats provide supplemental nutrition, like extra beet pulp and fiber to aid in digestion and weight maintenance.

Some people extend the "apples and carrots" scenario a bit further to "anything they happen to have handy," including sandwiches, soda, candy, and salty treats. Not all human food is intended to be eaten by horses, though. Chocolate is toxic to horses, and bread products can swell in the horse's esophagus and lead to a choking episode. Since horses can colic after eating the same meal every day, you may or may not feel comfortable finding out firsthand where your horse's tolerance level for human food is.

Many equestrians feel that the occasional treat tossed in the horse's feed bucket isn't a big deal. After all, humans tend to snack after a good workout, too.

On the other hand, some feel that a horse should receive positive reinforcement at the moment they are demonstrating good behavior. That may mean interrupting a ride or work session to distribute treats and praise. Opponents of treats feel there are different ways to offer your horse a reward for good performance, including vocal cues, like, "Good pony!" spoken in an enthusiastic, warm voice, or offering a pat or scratch along your horse's neck or withers if you're mounted. They feel that horses will learn to stop what they're doing to demand a treat any time they perform a task for which they've been rewarded in the past.

Many feel that a "pressure and release" system is more than adequate for explaining certain situations to horses. If a horse is raising their head and pulling on the lead rope when you're escorting them from paddock to stall, for example, many feel that the best way to teach a horse that this is unacceptable is to add a heavier lead rope or stud chain that will put extra pressure on a horse's face. When they stop pulling, the pressure releases and the handler or trainer can give the horse pats and verbal praise. Others feel that the point is not fully reinforced unless an incentive like a treat is offered. Some believe that giving a horse treats will make them more eager to perform correctly for their trainer or handler the first time.

Additional arguments against treats state that the added calories can cause weight gain and lead to insulin resistance, much as overindulging in food as a human has been found to correlate with an increase in health risks. Some feel that giving a horse too many treats is similar to giving a toddler too many sweets–while it may coax the desired behavior out of them, it can lead to an increased dependence on a less nutritional source of energy. Moderation and appropriate levels of exercise can mitigate these potential issues.

You will have to evaluate for yourself whether you think that treats are likely to turn your horse into a demanding, biting monster. You may choose to give your horses treats after a positive work session, at random, or whenever they do what you want them to do. You may decide at your horse can be trained to accept treats by hand or insist that treats are only provided in a safe feed dish. If you decide to allow treats, many people feel that it's important to monitor the amount, type, frequency, and delivery method of treats to ensure anyone who interacts with your horse respects these wishes.

As you explore training methods, experts, and opportunities, you will likely encounter some strong opinions on either side of these great debates. I encourage you to consider all sides and opinions and bear in mind that every horse is different.

Furthermore, I encourage you to keep an open mind and consider your own personal horse's behaviors and preferences when exploring different methods and techniques for dealing with inappropriate behavior in your horse. You are your horse's advocate. You are their voice, and you can tell a professional what you will and will not allow them to do with your horse. If you are boarding, make sure your barn owner and staff know your preferences so they can respect them as well.We all come from different backgrounds and experiences, just like our horses. When confronted with new training styles and mechanics, I encourage you to listen and get a feel for what's really being done before you decide whether or not that is a method that you support or advocate for your own horse.

Conclusion

So there you go: The secret to a well-mannered horse is lots of patience, observation, and making good choices! That may sound simple, but you might also discover that being a horse person is a lot more involved than you thought.

If your horse starts acting strangely seemingly overnight, I strongly urge you to call your vet first and foremost. Horses don't typically change personalities or develop bad habits immediately. There may be something physically inspiring this dramatic shift in attitude.

But, if your horse has always been a grumpy old cuss who tries to bite during the grooming and tacking-up process, that might just be established habits shining through. Many horses learn quickly that doing something drastic results in them getting exactly what they want, which is often "to be left alone eating grass and dozing in the sun."

Your horse may also be relying on their senses and instincts to tell them what's good and what's dangerous. Even the most well-trained horses can react to something strange to them. As part of your deal to be responsible for your horse's well-being, you are tasked with helping your horse understand that their reaction is inappropriate and guiding them towards making better choices.

You don't, however, have to do that alone. Asking for help from a medical or training professional can be beneficial for your growth as a horse person, and your horse's growth as a well-mannered equine. And, in some cases, you may need to evaluate if this is the right horse for you and the right home for your horse.

You may have noticed that I don't mention a lot of specific training methods or provide a lot of "how-to" information. I've received a few inquiries about that, and I'm not trying to hold out on amazing miracle-working magic. I try not to mention a lot of detail about horse training because I very much don't want someone to try my methods on their own horses, have it fail miserably for any reason, and feel like I have personally done something terrible to your horse.

Horse training includes a lot of observation, analysis, trying things, finding out they don't work, re-evaluating the situation, trying something different, and repeating all of these steps until something clicks and you and your horse are both on the same page. Sometimes this process takes 30 days, and sometimes you have less than 30 seconds to decide because a horse is about to go bonkers. The timing of both reward and punishment, positive and negative reinforcement, or pressure and release is imperative to training success. If you miss an opportunity, you have to wait until the stars align to recreate that moment. You can't force a horse to understand, there is no magic wand, and undoing a behavior that a horse has been doing for years may take just as long.

If I can't see your horse or learn from you what your horse is doing, I simply don't feel comfortable providing training advice. The area between "learning" and "making things worse" is simply too wide and too grey for me to blindly recommend an umbrella course of action through a book. There are things I have done with Red that would make a huge mess with Belle. Horses are just too different for everything to work perfectly the first time.

I recommend checking out some of the training sites in the Resources section to see which methods might jive best with you and your horse's personalities. Don't just watch one video from each trainer–binge-watch as many videos as you can! You may feel inspired to try some of the things you see in the videos with your horse, and I encourage it, as long as you feel safe and comfortable and do not take any unnecessary risks. If you are scared, skip it and go back to doing something familiar. You are not a failure. You are choosing the well-being of yourself and your horse.

A perfectly-behaved horse is hard to come by. I have never met a horse who was completely and utterly "bomb-proof," as we say. Some horses are more laid back about their surroundings, like Red. Some horses don't mind the activities occurring around them, as long as they aren't asked to do anything they don't want to do, like Belle. And there are horses for whom everything is new, exciting, and potentially dangerous. Like any other living being, horses can be a little different from day to day. Observing them carefully every day can help you decide which of their behaviors are learned, which are reactions that need to be redirected, and which may be signs that something's not quite right, or, "NQR" as my vet says.

I wish you all the best as you work with your equine buddy. I hope you have the patience you need to observe and understand the situation, the serenity to objectively make decisions for the next steps, and the clarity to know when you need to back off or get help. Horses are big, powerful, scary... wonderful, majestic, and cuddly. Any conversation you have with your horse about manners is going to take time, and you may have to repeat yourself a few times over the years. But, just like raising a child through those wildly unpredictable toddler years, those positive aspects of the relationship often shine through.

I hope this book and the resources that follow are helpful to you as you continue your journey with your horse. I wish you many fulfilling years in your partnership, with a few nips and "NO!"s, and plenty of pats and praise!

Resources

While I love sharing my knowledge and experiences with friends and readers, I recognize that I am not the final or only word when it comes to equine behavior, communication, or training. Therefore, I like to include a variety of perspectives on these topics.

I consider each of the following resources credible and worthy of reading and reflecting upon, but I also want to make it clear that I have no association with any of the people, websites, studies, resources, or entities included below. I don't want this to be construed as support, advocacy, or even agreement with any of the opinions discussed in these resources. This is merely a collection of links to publicly available websites and videos that help explain or demonstrate the points we've discussed in greater detail.

Since I can't answer every question you may have along the way, I thought it would be helpful to provide some very thorough resources! Click through with an open mind, and feel free to explore some of the publications or websites linked as well–many include a wealth of knowledge on a variety of topics.

Print Articles, PDFs, and Blogs

Lifestyle and Behavior Correlations

While I've covered this topic in a different book, the connection between horses' behavior and their contentment with their daily life is undeniable. These links lead to resources that can help you understand why your horse may be responding and reacting in certain ways, based on how they live.

Equus Magazine, "Are you setting your horse up for bad behavior?: https://equusmagazine.com/behavior/how-management-affects-behavior/

Horse and Rider blog, "4 Reasons Why Your Horse Is Too Hot to Handle"

https://horseandrider.com/blog/horse-too-hot-to-handle-anxious-nervous/

National Park Service (NPS) guide, "Wild Horse Behavior"

https://www.nps.gov/calo/learn/nature/upload/2007-Wild-Horse-Behavior.pdf

Nervous Behavior

The following resources may help those who are new to horses to better understand horse behavior. Each link focuses specifically on nervous behavior, which may help you better identify when your horse is being a brat, and when they are genuinely concerned.

Equus Magazine, "Do's and Don'ts in dealing with a nervous horse"

https://equusmagazine.com/behavior/dealing-with-a-nervous-horse/

Equine Helper, "Signs a Horse Is Anxious, Nervous, or Stressed"

https://equinehelper.com/signs-a-horse-is-stressed/

Horse Journals, "The Anxious Horse: Working Through Tension"
https://www.horsejournals.com/riding-training/general/schooling/anxious-horse-working-through-tension

Facial Expressions

Being able to read and understand your horse's facial expressions can be very helpful when understanding why they're acting out. These resources can help you better identify what your horse is thinking or feeling, based on their expressions and movement.

CNN.com, "Horses can make facial expressions just like humans"
https://www.cnn.com/2018/06/26/sport/horse-facial-expressions-spt/index.html

PLOS One research article, "Development and validation of the facial scale (FaceSed) to evaluate sedation in horses"
https://journals.plos.org/plosone/article?id=10.1371/journal.pone.0251909

The Hoof Blog, "Sue Dyson: Double video explanation of equine ethogram for recognizing lameness and pain"
https://hoofcare.blogspot.com/2017/06/sue-dyson-equine-ethogram-facial-expression-lameness-video.html

Body Language and Movement

Similarly, a horse's body language can tell us a lot about where a horse is both mentally and emotionally. These articles help identify and demonstrate the potential meaning behind different body movements and positioning.

Horse Illustrated magazine, "Equine Body Language"
https://www.horseillustrated.com/horse-keeping-horse-body-language

Horse Illustrated magazine, "How to Speak Horse"

https://www.horseillustrated.com/horse-keeping-how-to-speak-horse

Equine Wellness magazine, "Top 10 equine body language postures"

https://equinewellnessmagazine.com/top-10-body-language-postures/

Equine Spot website, "Understand Horse Body Language and You'll Unlock the Equine Communication Code"

https://www.equinespot.com/horse-body-language.html

Equus magazine, "What Your Horse's Tail Tells You"

https://equusmagazine.com/horse-care/horsetail_062206/

Horse Network, "Say What? A Quick Guide to Decoding Your Horse's Body Language"

https://horsenetwork.com/2017/05/say-what-a-quick-guide-to-decoding-your-horse-s-body-language/

Finding a Trainer

Finding a trainer can be a daunting task, no matter how many times you've successfully searched for one in the past. These sites offer some tips for finding, connecting with, and evaluating a trainer for your horse.

American Quarter Horse Association, "Find a Professional"

https://www.aqha.com/find-a-trainer1

Success Under Saddle Coaching, "How to Find an Exceptional Horse Trainer, Riding Instructor or Coach"

https://successundersaddle.com/how-to-find-an-exceptional-horse-trainer-riding-instructor-coach/

The Horse website, "Finding a Horse Trainer Who's Right for You (Or Your Child)" https://thehorse.com/167813/finding-a-horse-trainer-whos-right-for-you/

Horse and Rider magazine, " How (and Why) to Find a Trainer"

https://horseandrider.com/western-horse-training-tips/find-trainer-25708/

Horse Sales Sites

I strongly recommend exercising extreme willpower when perusing sales ads!

Equine.com

https://www.equine.com/

Dreamhorse.com

https://www.dreamhorse.com/

Horseclicks.com

https://www.horseclicks.com/

Foods That Horses Shouldn't Eat

For those who are curious about what "people food" horses can and cannot eat, these sites help explain the whats and whys.

Saddlebox gifts, "What Foods & Plants are Poisonous to Horses?"

https://www.saddlebox.net/what-foods-plants-are-poisonous-to-horses/

Horse Fact Book blog, "What Foods & Plants Are Harmful To Horses? 25 Things They Should NEVER Eat"

https://www.horsefactbook.com/guides/what-horses-should-never-eat/

Training Tools and How They Work

Some of the training tools mentioned throughout this book may be new to you, so I've included a few links to articles and a video that can help explain these tools and how they can be used to educate and inform a horse about their behavior.

US Whip product blog, "A Guide to Horse Training Tools, Whips, Crops"

https://uswhip.com/blog/a-guide-to-horse-training-tools-whips-crops/

Horse Journals magazine, "The Science of Tack and Training Aids"

https://www.horsejournals.com/riding-training/tack-gear/english/science-tack-and-training-aids

Thehorse.com, "Training Aid Fact and Fiction for Better Riding"

https://thehorse.com/182591/training-aid-fact-and-fiction-for-better-ridg/

Video: Larry Trocha, "Horse Training Aids: What they are & why use them"

https://www.youtube.com/watch?v=5RecmGz0Vss

Videos

Facial Expressions and Body Language

If you prefer a more detailed and largely visual exploration of how horses try to communicate with us, consider watching these videos. They may help you gain greater insight and appreciation for the subtleties of equine body language.

EquineHelper Channel, "READING HORSE BODY LANGUAGE AND BEHAVIOR" https://www.youtube.com/watch?v=I95J-kS7M0U

Spalding Labs Channel, "10 Equine Behaviors Explained by Dr. Robert M. Miller"

https://www.youtube.com/watch?v=bUiTv-ZzthQ

Mustang Maddy Channel, "How to Read Your Horse's Emotions"
https://www.youtube.com/watch?v=DSFfpmg1iR0

Behavior-Based Trainers

The following professionals are well-known trars with established methods, theories, and procedures. Remember that I'm not specifically agreeing with or advocating for any of these trainers, but I hope to present you with several different perspectives on training and behavioral issues. I encourage you to watch as many of these as you like to get a feel for all of the different tools and opportunities that exist to help your horse become a good citizen!

Monty Roberts - https://www.youtube.com/watch?v=smN9yebcibc

Clinton Anderson - https://www.youtube.com/watch?v=vZRLA7Ivh7Q

Pat Parelli - https://www.youtube.com/watch?v=aAFKxsjpyoY

Linda Tellington-Jones - https://www.youtube.com/watch?v=h9svZD5UKG4

John   Lyons   -
https://www.youtube.com/watch?v=zXGLMEpXAr0

Warwick Schiller - https://www.youtube.com/watch?v=qincE-Zod6mQ

West   Taylor   -
https://www.youtube.com/watch?v=bQag2hHFHq0

Sam   VanFleet   -
https://www.youtube.com/watch?v=5JyJ7ybG0fU

Download your free checklist now!

If you've ever checked out an equine supply website or stopped by a tack shop, you might find your head swimming regarding all of the stuff people buy to help them care for their horses. How do you decide what you need to buy?

I've created this checklist to help new horse owners get organized right from the start.

Go to https://free.meredithhillbook.com/checklist to download it for free

Review

Reviews and feedback help improve this book and the author. If you enjoy this book, we would greatly appreciate it if you could take a few moments to share your opinion and post a review on Amazon. Thank you!

Also By Meredith Hill

Finding Your First Horse: How to Buy a Horse without Losing Your Mind (or Money)

Before Your Horse Comes Home: Introductory Horse Care for Beginners

I Have a Horse... Now What: How Grooming, Training, Riding, and Equine Competitive Activities Can Build a Lifelong Bond

Help! I Bought a New Horse: What First -Time Horse Owners Need to Know About Grooming, Riding, Training, and Horse Care